P9-ARR-872

HEART OF THE CHRISTIAN LIFE

BENEDICT XVI

Heart of the
Christian Life

~

Thoughts on the Holy Mass

IGNATIUS PRESS   SAN FRANCISCO

Original German edition:
Herz des Christlichen Lebens: Gedanken zur Heiligen Messe
© 2008 by Sankt Ulrich Verlag, GmbH, Augsburg, Germany

Cover photograph of Pope Benedict XVI
by Stefano Spaziani

Cover design by Roxanne Mei Lum

© 2010 by Ignatius Press, San Francisco
ISBN 978-1-58617-432-3
Library of Congress Control Number 2009935081
Printed in the United States of America ∞

CONTENTS

THE BREAD OF LIFE

On the feast of Corpus Domini [Corpus Christi], the Church relives the mystery of Holy Thursday in the light of the Resurrection. There is also a Eucharistic procession on Holy Thursday, when the Church repeats the exodus of Jesus from the Upper Room to the Mount of Olives.

In Israel, the night of the Passover was celebrated in the home, within the intimacy of the family; this is how the first Passover in Egypt was commemorated, the night in which the blood of the paschal lamb, sprinkled on the crossbeam and doorposts of the houses, served as protection against the destroyer.

On that night, Jesus goes out and hands himself over to the betrayer, the destroyer, and in so doing, overcomes the night, overcomes the darkness of evil. Only in this way is the gift of the Eucharist, instituted in the Upper Room, fulfilled: Jesus truly gives his Body and his Blood. Crossing over the threshold of death, he becomes living Bread, true manna, endless nourishment for eternity. The flesh becomes the Bread of Life.

In the Holy Thursday procession, the Church accompanies Jesus to the Mount of Olives: it is the authentic desire of the Church in prayer to keep watch with Jesus, not to abandon him in the night of the world, on the night of betrayal, on the night of the indifference of many people.

On the feast of *Corpus Domini*, we again go on this procession, but in the joy of the Resurrection. The Lord is risen and leads us. In the narrations of the Resurrection there is a common and essential feature; the angels say: the Lord "goes ahead of you to Galilee, where you will see him" (Mt 28:7).

Taking this into deep consideration, we can say that this "going ahead" of Jesus implies a two-way direction.

The first is, as we have heard, Galilee. In Israel, Galilee was considered to be the doorway to the pagan world. And in reality, precisely on the mountain in Galilee, the disciples see Jesus, the Lord, who tells them: "Go . . . and make disciples of all the nations" (Mt 28:19).

The other preceding direction of the Risen One appears in the Gospel of Saint John, in the words of Jesus to Mary Magdalen: "Do not hold me, for I have not yet ascended to the Father" (Jn 20:17).

Jesus goes before us next to the Father, rises to the heights of God and invites us to follow him. These two directions on the Risen One's journey are not contradictory, for both indicate the path to follow Christ.

The true purpose of our journey is communion with God. He himself is the house of many dwelling places (cf. Jn 14:2ff.); but we can be elevated to these dwelling places only by going "toward Galilee", traveling on the pathways of the world, taking the Gospel to all nations, carrying the gift of his love to the men and women of all times.

Therefore, the journey of the Apostles extends to the "ends of the earth" (cf. Acts 1:6ff.). In this way, Saints Peter and Paul went all the way to Rome, a city that at that time was the center of the known world, the true *caput mundi*.

The Holy Thursday procession accompanies Jesus in his solitude toward the *via crucis*. The *Corpus Domini* procession responds instead in a symbolic way to the mandate of the Risen One: I go before you to Galilee. Go to the extreme ends of the world, take the Gospel to the world.

Of course, by faith, the Eucharist is an intimate mystery. The Lord instituted the Sacrament in the Upper Room, surrounded by his new family, by the Twelve Apostles, a prefiguration and anticipation of the Church of all times.

And so, in the liturgy of the ancient Church, the distribution of Holy Communion was introduced with the words *Sancta sanctis*: the holy gift is intended for those who have been made holy.

In this way a response was given to the exhortation of Saint Paul to the Corinthians: "A man should examine himself first; only then should he eat of the bread and drink of the cup . . ." (1 Cor 11:28).

Nevertheless, from this intimacy that is a most personal gift of the Lord, the strength of the Sacrament of the Eucharist goes above and beyond the walls of our Churches. In this Sacrament, the Lord is always journeying to meet the world. This universal aspect of the Eucharistic presence becomes evident in today's festive procession.

We bring Christ, present under the sign of bread, onto the streets of our city. We entrust these streets, these homes, our daily life, to his goodness. May our streets be streets of Jesus! May our houses be homes for him and with him! May our life of every day be penetrated by his presence.

With this gesture, let us place under his eyes the sufferings of the sick, the solitude of young people and the elderly, temptations, fears—our entire life. The procession represents an immense and public blessing for our city: Christ is, in person, the divine Blessing for the world. May the ray of his blessing extend to us all!

Our procession finishes in front of the Basilica of Saint

Mary Major in the encounter with Our Lady, called by the dear Pope John Paul II, "Woman of the Eucharist". Mary, Mother of the Lord, truly teaches us what entering into communion with Christ is: Mary offered her own flesh, her own blood to Jesus and became a living tent of the Word, allowing herself to be penetrated by his presence in body and spirit.

Let us pray to her, our holy Mother, so that she may help us to open our entire being, always more, to Christ's presence; so that she may help us to follow him faithfully, day after day, on the streets of our life. Amen!

WITHOUT SUNDAY WE CANNOT LIVE

"Glorify the Lord, Jerusalem; Zion, praise your God" (Responsorial Psalm).

The invitation of the Psalmist that is also echoed in the Sequence expresses very clearly the meaning of this Eucharistic Celebration: we are gathered here to praise and bless the Lord. This is what urged the Italian Church to gather here in Bari on the occasion of the National Eucharistic Congress.

I also wanted to join all of you today to give special emphasis to the celebration of the Solemnity of the Body and Blood of Christ, thus to pay homage to Christ in the Sacrament of his love and at the same time to strengthen the bonds of communion that bind me to the Church in Italy and to her Pastors. My venerable and beloved Predecessor, Pope John Paul II, would also have liked to have been here at this important ecclesial event, as you know. We all feel that he is close to us and with us is glorifying Christ, the Good Shepherd, whom he can now contemplate directly.

I greet with affection all of you who are taking part in this solemn liturgy: Cardinal Camillo Ruini and the other Cardinals present, Archbishop Francesco Cacucci of Bari, whom I thank for his kind words, the Bishops of Puglia and those who have come here in large numbers from every corner of Italy; priests, men and women religious and lay people, particularly the young people, and of course, all those who helped in various ways with the organization of the Congress.

I likewise greet the Authorities who, with their welcome presence, stress that Eucharistic Congresses are part of the history and culture of the Italian people.

The intention of this Eucharistic Congress, which ends today, was once again to present Sunday as the "weekly Easter", an expression of the identity of the Christian community and the center of its life and mission.

The chosen theme—*"Without Sunday we cannot live"*— takes us back to the year 304, when the Emperor Diocletian forbade Christians, on pain of death, from possessing the Scriptures, from gathering on Sundays to celebrate the Eucharist and from building places in which to hold their assemblies.

In Abitene, a small village in present-day Tunisia, forty-nine Christians were taken by surprise one Sunday while they were celebrating the Eucharist, gathered in the house of Octavius Felix, thereby defying the imperial prohibitions. They were arrested and taken to Carthage to be interrogated by the Proconsul Anulinus.

Significant among other things is the answer a certain Emeritus gave to the Proconsul who asked him why on earth they had disobeyed the Emperor's severe orders. He replied: *"Sine dominico non possumus"*: that is, we cannot live without joining together on Sunday to celebrate the Eucharist. We would lack the strength to face our daily problems and not to succumb.

After atrocious tortures, these forty-nine martyrs of Abitene were killed. Thus, they confirmed their faith with bloodshed. They died, but they were victorious: today we remember them in the glory of the Risen Christ.

The experience of the martyrs of Abitene is also one on

which we twenty-first-century Christians should reflect. It is not easy for us either to live as Christians, even if we are spared such prohibitions from the emperor. From a spiritual point of view, the world in which we find ourselves, often marked by unbridled consumerism, religious indifference and a secularism closed to transcendence, can appear a desert just as "vast and terrible" (Dt 8:15) as the one we heard about in the first reading from the Book of Deuteronomy. God came to the aid of the Jewish people in difficulty in this desert with his gift of manna, to make them understand that "not by bread alone does man live, but by every word that comes forth from the mouth of the Lord" (Dt 8:3).

In today's Gospel, Jesus has explained to us, through the gift of manna, for what bread God wanted to prepare the people of the New Covenant. Alluding to the Eucharist he said: "This is the bread that came down from heaven. Unlike your ancestors who ate and died nonetheless, the man who feeds on this bread shall live forever" (Jn 6:58).

In taking flesh, the Son of God could become Bread and thus be the nourishment of his people, of us, journeying on in this world toward the promised land of heaven.

We need this Bread to face the fatigue and weariness of our journey. Sunday, the Lord's Day, is a favorable opportunity to draw strength from him, the Lord of life.

The Sunday precept is not, therefore, an externally imposed duty, a burden on our shoulders. On the contrary, taking part in the Celebration, being nourished by the Eucharistic Bread and experiencing the communion of their brothers and sisters in Christ is a need for Christians, it is a joy; Christians can thus replenish the energy they need to continue on the journey we must make every week.

Moreover, this is not an arbitrary journey: the path God

points out to us through his Word goes in the direction inscribed in man's very existence. The Word of God and reason go together. For the human being, following the Word of God, going with Christ means fulfilling oneself; losing it is equivalent to losing oneself.

The Lord does not leave us alone on this journey. He is with us; indeed, he wishes to share our destiny to the point of identifying with us.

In the Gospel discourse that we have just heard he says, "He who feeds on my flesh and drinks my blood remains in me, and I in him" (Jn 6:56). How is it possible not to rejoice in such a promise?

However, we have heard that at his first announcement, instead of rejoicing, the people started to murmur in protest: "How can he give us his flesh to eat?" (Jn 6:52). To tell the truth, that attitude has frequently been repeated in the course of history. One might say that basically people do not want to have God so close, to be so easily within reach or to share so deeply in the events of their daily life.

Rather, people want him to be great and, in brief, we also often want him to be a little distant from us. Questions are then raised that are intended to show that, after all, such closeness would be impossible.

But the words that Christ spoke on that occasion have lost none of their clarity: "Let me solemnly assure you, if you do not eat the flesh of the Son of Man and drink his blood, you have no life in you" (Jn 6:53). Truly, we need a God who is close to us. In the face of the murmur of protest, Jesus might have fallen back on reassuring words: "Friends", he could have said, "do not worry! I spoke of flesh but it is only a symbol. What I mean is only a deep communion of sentiments."

But no, Jesus did not have recourse to such soothing

words. He stuck to his assertion, to all his realism, even when he saw many of his disciples breaking away (cf. Jn 6:66). Indeed, he showed his readiness to accept even desertion by his apostles, while not in any way changing the substance of his discourse: "Do you want to leave me too?" (Jn 6:67), he asked. Thanks be to God, Peter's response was one that even we can make our own today with full awareness: "Lord, to whom shall we go? You have the words of eternal life" (Jn 6:68). We need a God who is close, a God who puts himself in our hands and who loves us.

Christ is truly present among us in the Eucharist. His presence is not static. It is a dynamic presence that grasps us, to make us his own, to make us assimilate him. Christ draws us to himself, he makes us come out of ourselves to make us all one with him. In this way he also integrates us in the communities of brothers and sisters, and communion with the Lord is always also communion with our brothers and sisters. And we see the beauty of this communion that the Blessed Eucharist gives us.

We are touching on a further dimension of the Eucharist that I would like to point out before concluding.

The Christ whom we meet in the Sacrament is the same here in Bari as he is in Rome, here in Europe, as in America, Africa, Asia and Oceania. He is the one same Christ who is present in the Eucharistic Bread of every place on earth. This means that we can encounter him only together with all others. We can only receive him in unity.

Is not this what the Apostle Paul said in the reading we have just heard? In writing to the Corinthians he said: "Because the loaf of bread is one, we, many though we are, are one body, for we all partake of the one loaf" (1 Cor 10:17).

The consequence is clear: we cannot communicate with the Lord if we do not communicate with one another. If we want to present ourselves to him, we must also take a step toward meeting one another.

To do this we must learn the great lesson of forgiveness: we must not let the gnawings of resentment work in our soul, but must open our hearts to the magnanimity of listening to others, open our hearts to understanding them, eventually to accepting their apologies, to generously offering our own.

The Eucharist, let us repeat, is the sacrament of unity. Unfortunately, however, Christians are divided, precisely in the sacrament of unity. Sustained by the Eucharist, we must feel all the more roused to striving with all our strength for that full unity which Christ ardently desired in the Upper Room.

Precisely here in Bari, fortunate Bari, a city that preserves the bones of Saint Nicholas, a land of encounter and dialogue with our Christian brethren of the East, I would like to reaffirm my desire to assume as a fundamental commitment working with all my might for the re-establishment of the full and visible unity of all Christ's followers.

I am aware that expressions of good will do not suffice for this. We need concrete acts that penetrate souls and shake consciences, prompting each one to that inner conversion that is the necessary condition for any progress on the path of ecumenism (cf. Message to the Universal Church, Sistine Chapel, 20 April 2005; *L'Osservatore Romano* English Edition, 27 April, p. 3).

I ask you all to set out with determination on the path of that spiritual ecumenism which, through prayer, opens the doors to the Holy Spirit, who alone can create unity.

Dear friends who have come to Bari from various parts of Italy to celebrate this Eucharistic Congress, we must rediscover the joy of Christian Sundays. We must proudly rediscover the privilege of sharing in the Eucharist, which is the sacrament of the renewed world.

Christ's Resurrection happened on the first day of the week, which in the Scriptures is the day of the world's creation. For this very reason Sunday was considered by the early Christian community as the day on which the new world began, the one on which, with Christ's victory over death, the new creation began.

As they gathered round the Eucharistic table, the community was taking shape as a new people of God. Saint Ignatius of Antioch described Christians as "having attained new hope" and presented them as people "who lived in accordance with Sunday" ("*iuxta dominicam viventes*"). In this perspective, the Bishop of Antioch wondered: "How will we be able to live without him, the One whom the prophets so long awaited?" (*Ep. ad Magnesios*, 9, 1–2).

"How will we be able to live without him?" In these words of Saint Ignatius we hear echoing the affirmation of the martyrs of Abitene: "*Sine dominico non possumus.*"

It is this that gives rise to our prayer: that we too, Christians of today, will rediscover an awareness of the crucial importance of the Sunday Celebration and will know how to draw from participation in the Eucharist the necessary dynamism for a new commitment to proclaiming to the world Christ "our peace" (Eph 2:14). Amen!

MARY, THE EUCHARISTIC WOMAN

I join you with great joy at the end of this prayer meeting organized by the Vicariate of Vatican City. I note with pleasure that a large number of you have gathered in the Vatican Gardens for the conclusion of the month of May. Among you, in particular, are many people who live or work in the Vatican, with their families. I offer a warm greeting to you all; in a special way the Cardinals and Bishops, beginning with Archbishop Angelo Comastri who has led this prayer meeting. I then greet the priests and the men and women religious present, with a thought also for the contemplative Sisters of *Mater Ecclesiae* Monastery who are spiritually united to us.

Dear friends, you have wound your way up to the Grotto of Lourdes reciting the holy Rosary, as if to respond to the Virgin's invitation to raise your spirit toward heaven. Our Lady accompanies us every day in our prayers. During this special Year of the Eucharist in which we are living, Mary helps us above all to discover ever better the great sacrament of the Eucharist.

In his last Encyclical, *Ecclesia de Eucharistia*, our beloved Pope John Paul II presented her to us as "Woman of the Eucharist" throughout her life (cf. no. 53). "Woman of the Eucharist" through and through, beginning with her inner disposition: from the Annunciation, when she offered herself for the Incarnation of the Word of God, to the Cross and to the Resurrection; "Woman of the Eucharist" in the period subsequent to Pentecost, when she received in the Sacrament that Body which she had conceived and carried in her womb.

Today, in particular, we pause to meditate on the mystery of the Visitation of the Virgin to Saint Elizabeth. Mary went to see her elderly cousin Elizabeth, whom everyone said was sterile but who instead had reached the sixth month of a pregnancy given to her by God (cf. Lk 1:36), carrying in her womb the recently conceived Jesus. She was a young girl but she was not afraid, for God was with her, within her.

In a certain way we can say that her journey was—we like to emphasize in this Year of the Eucharist—the first "Eucharistic procession" in history. Mary, living Tabernacle of God made flesh, is the Ark of the Covenant in whom the Lord visited and redeemed his people. Jesus' presence filled her with the Holy Spirit.

When she entered Elizabeth's house, her greeting was overflowing with grace: John leapt in his mother's womb, as if he were aware of the coming of the One whom he would one day proclaim to Israel. The children exulted, the mothers exulted. This meeting, imbued with the joy of the Holy Spirit, is expressed in the Canticle of the *Magnificat*.

Is this not also the joy of the Church, which ceaselessly welcomes Christ in the holy Eucharist and brings him into the world with the testimony of active charity, steeped in faith and hope? Yes, welcoming Jesus and bringing him to others is the true joy of Christians!

Dear Brothers and Sisters, let us follow and imitate Mary, a deeply Eucharistic soul, and our whole life can become a *Magnificat* (cf. *Ecclesia de Eucharistia*, no. 58), praise of God. May this be the grace that we ask from the Virgin Most Holy this evening at the end of the month of May. My Blessing to you all.

IN THE HOUR OF JESUS

In the presence of the Sacred Host, in which Jesus becomes for us the bread that sustains and feeds us (cf. Jn 6:35), and there we began our inner journey of adoration. In the Eucharist, adoration must become union.

At the celebration of the Eucharist, we find ourselves in the "hour" of Jesus, to use the language of John's Gospel. Through the Eucharist this "hour" of Jesus becomes our own hour, his presence in our midst. Together with the disciples he celebrated the Passover of Israel, the memorial of God's liberating action that led Israel from slavery to freedom. Jesus follows the rites of Israel. He recites over the bread the prayer of praise and blessing.

But then something new happens. He thanks God not only for the great works of the past; he thanks him for his own exaltation, soon to be accomplished through the Cross and Resurrection, and he speaks to the disciples in words that sum up the whole of the Law and the Prophets: "This is my Body, given in sacrifice for you. This cup is the New Covenant in my Blood." He then distributes the bread and the cup, and instructs them to repeat his words and actions of that moment over and over again in his memory.

What is happening? How can Jesus distribute his Body and his Blood?

By making the bread into his Body and the wine into his Blood, he anticipates his death, he accepts it in his heart, and he transforms it into an action of love. What on the outside is simply brutal violence—the Crucifixion—from within becomes an act of total self-giving love. This is the substantial transformation which was accomplished at the Last Supper and was destined to set in motion a series of transformations leading ultimately to the transformation of the world when God will be all in all (cf. 1 Cor 15:28).

In their hearts, people always and everywhere have somehow expected a change, a transformation of the world. Here now is the central act of transformation that alone can truly renew the world: violence is transformed into love, and death into life.

Since this act transmutes death into love, death as such is already conquered from within, the Resurrection is already present in it. Death is, so to speak, mortally wounded, so that it can no longer have the last word.

To use an image well known to us today, this is like inducing nuclear fission in the very heart of being—the victory of love over hatred, the victory of love over death. Only this intimate explosion of good conquering evil can then trigger off the series of transformations that little by little will change the world.

All other changes remain superficial and cannot save. For this reason we speak of redemption: what had to happen at the most intimate level has indeed happened, and we can enter into its dynamic. Jesus can distribute his Body, because he truly gives himself.

This first fundamental transformation of violence into love, of death into life, brings other changes in its wake. Bread and wine become his Body and Blood.

But it must not stop there; on the contrary, the process of transformation must now gather momentum. The Body and Blood of Christ are given to us so that we ourselves will be transformed in our turn. We are to become the Body of Christ, his own Flesh and Blood.

We all eat the one bread, and this means that we ourselves become one. In this way, adoration, as we said earlier, becomes union. God no longer simply stands before us as the One who is totally Other. He is within us, and we are in him. His dynamic enters into us and then seeks to spread outward to others until it fills the world, so that his love can truly become the dominant measure of the world.

I like to illustrate this new step urged upon us by the Last Supper by drawing out the different nuances of the word "adoration" in Greek and in Latin. The Greek word is *proskynesis*. It refers to the gesture of submission, the recognition of God as our true measure, supplying the norm that we choose to follow. It means that freedom is not simply about enjoying life in total autonomy, but rather about living by the measure of truth and goodness, so that we ourselves can become true and good. This gesture is necessary even if initially our yearning for freedom makes us inclined to resist it.

We can only fully accept it when we take the second step that the Last Supper proposes to us. The Latin word for adoration is *ad-oratio*—mouth to mouth contact, a kiss, an embrace, and hence, ultimately love. Submission becomes union, because he to whom we submit is Love. In this way submission acquires a meaning, because it does not impose anything on us from the outside, but liberates us deep within.

Let us return once more to the Last Supper. The new element to emerge here was the deeper meaning given to Israel's ancient prayer of blessing, which from that point on became the word of transformation, enabling us to participate in the "hour" of Christ. Jesus did not instruct us to repeat the Passover meal, which in any event, given that it is an anniversary, is not repeatable at will. He instructed us to enter into his "hour".

We enter into it through the sacred power of the words of consecration—a transformation brought about through the prayer of praise which places us in continuity with Israel and the whole of salvation history, and at the same time ushers in the new, to which the older prayer at its deepest level was pointing.

The new prayer—which the Church calls the "Eucharistic Prayer"—brings the Eucharist into being. It is the word of power which transforms the gifts of the earth in an entirely new way into God's gift of himself, and it draws us into this process of transformation. That is why we call this action "Eucharist", which is a translation of the Hebrew word *berakha*—thanksgiving, praise, blessing, and a transformation worked by the Lord: the presence of his "hour". Jesus' hour is the hour in which love triumphs. In other words: it is God who has triumphed, because he is Love.

Jesus' hour seeks to become our own hour and will indeed become so if we allow ourselves, through the celebration of the Eucharist, to be drawn into that process of transformation that the Lord intends to bring about. The Eucharist must become the center of our lives.

If the Church tells us that the Eucharist is an essential part of Sunday, this is no mere positivism or thirst for power. On Easter morning, first the women and then the disciples had the grace of seeing the Lord. From that moment on, they knew that the first day of the week, Sunday, would be his day, the day of Christ the Lord. The day when creation began became the day when creation was renewed. Creation and redemption belong together. That is why Sunday is so important.

It is good that today, in many cultures, Sunday is a free day, and is often combined with Saturday so as to constitute a "week-end" of free time. Yet this free time is empty if God is not present.

Dear friends! Sometimes, our initial impression is that having to include time for Mass on a Sunday is rather inconvenient. But if you make the effort, you will realize that this is what gives a proper focus to your free time.

Do not be deterred from taking part in Sunday Mass, and help others to discover it too. This is because the Eucharist releases the joy that we need so much, and we must learn to grasp it ever more deeply, we must learn to love it.

Let us pledge ourselves to do this—it is worth the effort! Let us discover the intimate riches of the Church's liturgy and its true greatness: it is not we who are celebrating for ourselves, but it is the living God himself who is preparing a banquet for us.

Through your love for the Eucharist you will also rediscover the Sacrament of Reconciliation, in which the merciful goodness of God always allows us to make a fresh start in our lives.

Anyone who has discovered Christ must lead others to him. A great joy cannot be kept to oneself. It has to be passed on.

In vast areas of the world today there is a strange forgetfulness of God. It seems as if everything would be just the same even without him.

But at the same time there is a feeling of frustration, a sense of dissatisfaction with everyone and everything.

People tend to exclaim: "This cannot be what life is about!" Indeed not. And so, together with forgetfulness of

God there is a kind of new explosion of religion. I have no wish to discredit all the manifestations of this phenomenon. There may be sincere joy in the discovery. But to tell the truth, religion often becomes almost a consumer product. People choose what they like, and some are even able to make a profit from it.

But religion sought on a "do-it-yourself" basis cannot ultimately help us. It may be comfortable, but at times of crisis we are left to ourselves.

Help people to discover the true star which points out the way to us: Jesus Christ! Let us seek to know him better and better, so as to be able to guide others to him with conviction.

This is why love for Sacred Scripture is so important, and in consequence, it is important to know the faith of the Church which opens up for us the meaning of Scripture. It is the Holy Spirit who guides the Church as her faith grows, causing her to enter ever more deeply into the truth (cf. Jn 16:13).

Beloved Pope John Paul II gave us a wonderful work in which the faith of centuries is explained synthetically: the *Catechism of the Catholic Church*. I myself recently presented the *Compendium* of the *Catechism*, also prepared at the request of the late Holy Father. These are two fundamental texts which I recommend to all of you.

Obviously books alone are not enough. Form communities based on faith!

In recent decades, movements and communities have come to birth in which the power of the Gospel is keenly felt. Seek communion in faith, like fellow travelers who continue together to follow the path of the great pilgrimage that the Magi from the East first pointed out to us. The spontaneity of new communities is important, but it is also important to preserve communion with the Pope and with the Bishops. It is they who guarantee that we are not seeking private paths, but instead are living as God's great family, founded by the Lord through the Twelve Apostles.

Once again, I must return to the Eucharist. "Because there is one bread, we, though many, are one body", says Saint Paul (1 Cor 10:17). By this he meant: since we receive the same Lord and he gathers us together and draws us into himself, we ourselves are one.

This must be evident in our lives. It must be seen in our capacity to forgive. It must be seen in our sensitivity to the needs of others. It must be seen in our willingness to share. It must be seen in our commitment to our neighbors, both those close at hand and those physically far away, whom we nevertheless consider to be close.

Today, there are many forms of voluntary assistance, models of mutual service, of which our society has urgent need. We must not, for example, abandon the elderly to their solitude, we must not pass by when we meet people who are suffering. If we think and live according to our communion with Christ, then our eyes will be opened. Then we will no longer be content to scrape a living just for ourselves, but we will see where and how we are needed.

Living and acting thus, we will soon realize that it is much better to be useful and at the disposal of others than to be concerned only with the comforts that are offered to us.

I know that you as young people have great aspirations, that you want to pledge yourselves to build a better world. Let others see this, let the world see it, since this is exactly the witness that the world expects from the disciples of Jesus Christ; in this way, and through your love above all, the world will be able to discover the star that we follow as believers.

Let us go forward with Christ and let us live our lives as true worshippers of God!

THE WINE OF TRUE LOVE

The reading from the Prophet Isaiah and today's Gospel set before our eyes one of the great images of Sacred Scripture: the image of the vine. In Sacred Scripture, bread represents all that human beings need for their daily life. Water makes the earth fertile: it is the fundamental gift that makes life possible. Wine, on the other hand, expresses the excellence of creation and gives us the feast in which we go beyond the limits of our daily routine: wine, the Psalm says, "gladdens the heart". So it is that wine and with it the vine have also become images of the gift of love in which we can taste the savor of the Divine. Thus, the reading from the Prophet that we have just heard begins like a canticle of love: God created a vineyard for himself—this is an image of the history of love for humanity, of his love for Israel which he chose. This is therefore the first thought in today's readings: God instilled in men and women, created in his image, the capacity for love, hence also the capacity for loving him, their Creator. With the Prophet Isaiah's canticle of love God wants to speak to the hearts of his people— and to each one of us. "I have created you in my image and likeness", he says to us. "I myself am love and you are my image to the extent that the splendor of love shines out in you, to the extent that you respond lovingly to me." God is waiting for us. He wants us to love him: should not our hearts be moved by this appeal? At this very moment when we are celebrating the Eucharist, in which we are opening the Synod on the Eucharist, he comes to meet us, he comes to meet me. Will he find a response? Or will what happened to the vine of which God says in Isaiah: "He waited for it to produce grapes but it yielded wild grapes", also happen to us? Is not our Christian life often far more like vinegar than wine? Self-pity, conflict, indifference?

With this we have automatically come to the second fundamental thought in today's readings. As we have heard, they speak first of all of the goodness of God's creation and of the greatness of the choice by which he seeks us out and loves us. But they then also speak of the story that was successively lived out—of the "fall" of man. God had planted the very best vines, yet they yielded wild grapes. Let us ask ourselves: what do wild grapes consist of? The good grapes that God was hoping for, the Prophet sings, would have been justice and righteousness. Wild grapes instead bring violence, bloodshed and oppression that make people groan under the yoke of injustice. In the Gospel, the image changes: the vine produces good grapes, but the tenants keep them for themselves. They are not willing to hand them over to the owner of the vineyard. They beat and kill his messengers and kill his son. Their motive is simple: they themselves want to become owners; they take possession of what does not belong to them. In the foreground of the Old Testament is the accusation of the violation of social justice, of contempt for human beings by human beings. In the background, however, it appears that with contempt for the Torah, for the law given by God, it is God himself who is despised. All people want is to enjoy their own power. This aspect is fully highlighted in Jesus' Parable: the tenants do not want to have a master—and these tenants are also a mirror of ourselves. We men and women, to whom creation is as it were entrusted for its management, have usurped it. We ourselves want to dominate it in the first person and by ourselves. We want unlimited possession of the world and of our own lives. God is in our way. Either he is reduced merely to a few devout words, or he is denied in everything and banned from public life so as to lose all meaning. The tolerance that admits God as it were as a private opinion but refuses him the public domain, the reality of the world and of our lives, is not tolerance but hypocrisy. But nowhere that the human being makes himself the one lord of the world and owner of himself can justice exist. There, it is only the desire for power and private interests that can prevail. Of course, one can chase the Son out of the vineyard and kill him, in order selfishly to taste the fruits of the earth alone. However, in no time at all the vineyard then reverts to being an uncultivated piece of land, trampled by wild boar as the Responsorial Psalm tells us (cf. Ps 80[79]:14).

Thus, we reach a third element of today's readings. In the Old and New Testaments, the Lord proclaims judgment on the unfaithful vineyard. The judgment that Isaiah foresaw is brought about in the great wars and exiles for which the Assyrians and Babylonians were responsible. The judgment announced by the Lord Jesus refers above all to the destruction of Jerusalem in the year 70. Yet the threat of judgment also concerns us, the Church in Europe, Europe and the West in general. With this Gospel, the Lord is also crying out to our ears the words that in the Book of Revelation he addresses to the Church of Ephesus: "If you do not repent I will come to you and remove your lampstand from its place" (2:5). Light can also be taken away from us and we do well to let this warning ring out with its full seriousness in our hearts, while crying to the Lord: "Help us to repent! Give all of us the grace of true renewal! Do not allow your light in our midst to blow out! Strengthen our faith, our hope and our love, so that we can bear good fruit!"

At this point, however, we ask ourselves: "But is there no promise, no word of comfort in today's readings and Gospel? Is the threat the last word?" No! There is a promise, and this is the last, the essential word. We hear it in the Alleluia verse from John's Gospel: "I am the vine, you are the branches. He who lives in me and I in him will produce abundantly" (Jn 15:5). With these words of the Lord, John illustrates for us the final, true outcome of the history of God's vineyard. God does not fail. In the end he wins, love wins. A veiled allusion to this can already be found in the Parable of the Tenants presented by today's Gospel and in the concluding words. There too, the death of the Son is not the end of history, even if the rest of the story is not directly recounted. But Jesus expresses this death through a new image taken from the Psalm: "The stone which the builders rejected has become the cornerstone . . ." (cf. Mt 21:42; Ps 118[117]:22). From the Son's death springs life, a new building is raised, a new vineyard. He, who at Cana changed water into wine, has transformed his Blood into the wine of true love and thus transforms the wine into his Blood. In the Upper Room he anticipated his death and transformed it into the gift of himself in an act of radical love. His Blood is a gift, it is love, and consequently it is the true wine that the Creator was expecting. In this way, Christ himself became the vine, and this vine always bears good fruit: the presence of his love for us which is indestructible.

These parables thus lead at the end to the mystery of the Eucharist, in which the Lord gives us the bread of life and the wine of his love and invites us to the banquet of his eternal love. We celebrate the Eucharist in the awareness that its price was the death of the Son—the sacrifice of his life that remains present in it. Every time we eat this bread and drink this cup, we proclaim the death of the Lord until he comes, Saint Paul says (cf. 1 Cor 11:26). But we also know that from this death springs life, because Jesus transformed it into a sacrificial gesture, an act of love, thereby profoundly changing it: love has overcome death. In the Holy Eucharist, from the Cross, he draws us all to himself (cf. Jn 12:32) and makes us branches of the Vine that is Christ himself. If we abide in him, we will also bear fruit, and then from us will no longer come the vinegar of self-sufficiency, of dissatisfaction with God and his creation, but the good wine of joy in God and of love for our neighbor. Let us pray to the Lord to give us his grace, so that in the three weeks of the Synod which we are about to begin, not only will we say beautiful things about the Eucharist but above all, we will live from its power. Let us invoke this gift through Mary, dear Synod Fathers whom I greet with deep affection as well as the various Communities from which you come and which you represent here, so that, docile to the action of the Holy Spirit, we may help the world become in Christ and with Christ the fruitful vine of God. Amen.

THE EUCHARIST AS
THE WAY TO HOLINESS

Today's liturgy invites us to contemplate the Eucharist as the source of holiness and spiritual nourishment for our mission in the world: this supreme "gift and mystery" manifests and communicates to us the fullness of God's love.

The Word of the Lord, just proclaimed in the Gospel, has reminded us that all of divine law is summed up in love. The dual commandment to love God and neighbor contains the two aspects of a single dynamism of the heart and of life. Jesus thus brings to completion the ancient revelation, not by adding an unheard-of commandment, but by realizing in himself and in his work of salvation the living synthesis of the two great commands of the Old Covenant: "You shall love the Lord your God with your whole heart . . ." and "You shall love your neighbor as yourself" (cf. Dt 6:5; Lv 19:18).

In the Eucharist we contemplate the Sacrament of this living synthesis of the law: Christ offers to us, in himself, the complete fulfillment of love for God and love for our brothers and sisters. He communicates his love to us when we are nourished by his Body and Blood.

In this way, Saint Paul's words to the Thessalonians in today's Second Reading are brought to completion in us: "You turned to God from idols, to serve him who is the living and true God" (1 Thes 1:9). This conversion is the beginning of the walk of holiness that the Christian is called to achieve in his own life.

The saint is the person who is so fascinated by the beauty of God and by his perfect truth as to be progressively transformed by it. Because of this beauty and truth, he is ready to renounce everything, even himself. Love of God is enough for him, experienced in humble and disinterested service to one's neighbor, especially toward those who cannot give back in return. . . .

Contemplation of the Eucharist must urge all the members of the Church, priests in the first place, ministers of the Eucharist, to revive their commitment of faithfulness. The celibacy that priests have received as a precious gift and the sign of undivided love toward God and neighbor is founded upon the mystery of the Eucharist, celebrated and adored.

For lay persons too, Eucharistic spirituality must be the interior motor of every activity, and no dichotomy is acceptable between faith and life in their mission of spreading the spirit of Christianity in the world.

With the closing of the Year of the Eucharist, how can we not give thanks to God for the many gifts granted to the Church during this time? And how can we not take up once again the invitation of our beloved Pope John Paul II to "start afresh from Christ"?

Like the disciples of Emmaus, whose hearts were kindled by the words of the Risen One and enlightened by his living presence recognized in the breaking of the bread, who hurriedly returned to Jerusalem and became messengers of Christ's Resurrection, we too must take up the path again, enlivened by the fervent desire to witness to the mystery of this love that gives hope to the world.

It is in this Eucharistic perspective that today's World Mission Sunday is well situated, to which the venerated Servant of God John Paul II gave as the theme for reflection: *Mission: bread broken for the life of the world.*

When the Ecclesial Community celebrates the Eucharist, especially on Sunday, the Day of the Lord, it better understands that Christ's sacrifice is "for all" (Mt 26:28), and that the Eucharist urges Christians to be "bread broken" for others, to commit themselves to a more just and fraternal world.

Even today, faced with the crowds, Christ continues to exhort his disciples: "Give them something to eat yourselves" (Mt 14:16), and in his Name, missionaries proclaim and witness to the Gospel, sometimes with the sacrifice of their lives.

Dear friends, we must all start afresh from the Eucharist. Mary, Woman of the Eucharist, will help us to "fall in love" with it, she will help us to "remain" in Christ's love, to be deeply renewed by him.

Docile to the Spirit's action and attentive to the needs of others, the Church will be evermore a beacon of light, of true joy and hope, fully achieving its mission as "sign and instrument . . . of unity among all men" (*Lumen Gentium*, no. 1).

JESUS CHRIST:
INCARNATE LOVE OF GOD

12. (. . .) The real novelty of the New Testament lies not so much in new ideas as in the figure of Christ himself, who gives flesh and blood to those concepts—an unprecedented realism. In the Old Testament, the novelty of the Bible did not consist merely in abstract notions but in God's unpredictable and in some sense unprecedented activity. This divine activity now takes on dramatic form when, in Jesus Christ, it is God himself who goes in search of the "stray sheep", a suffering and lost humanity. When Jesus speaks in his parables of the shepherd who goes after the lost sheep, of the woman who looks for the lost coin, of the father who goes to meet and embrace his prodigal son, these are no mere words: they constitute an explanation of his very being and activity. His death on the Cross is the culmination of that turning of God against himself in which he gives himself in order to raise man up and save him. This is love in its most radical form. By contemplating the pierced side of Christ (cf. 19:37), we can understand the starting-point of this Encyclical Letter: "God is love" (1 Jn 4:8). It is there that this truth can be contemplated. It is from there that our definition of love must begin. In this contemplation the Christian discovers the path along which his life and love must move.

13. Jesus gave this act of oblation an enduring presence through his institution of the Eucharist at the Last Supper. He anticipated his death and resurrection by giving his disciples, in the bread and wine, his very self, his Body and Blood as the new manna (cf. Jn 6:31–33). The ancient world had dimly perceived that man's real food—what truly nourishes him as man—is ultimately the *Logos*, eternal wisdom: this same *Logos* now truly becomes food for us—as love. The Eucharist draws us into Jesus' act of self-oblation. More than just statically receiving the incarnate *Logos*, we enter into the very dynamic of his self-giving. The imagery of marriage between God and Israel is now realized in a way previously inconceivable: it had meant standing in God's presence, but now it becomes union with God through sharing in Jesus' self-gift, sharing in his Body and Blood. The sacramental "mysticism", grounded in God's condescension toward us, operates at a radically different level and lifts us to far greater heights than anything that any human mystical elevation could ever accomplish.

14. Here we need to consider yet another aspect: this sacramental "mysticism" is social in character, for in sacramental communion I become one with the Lord, like all the other communicants. As Saint Paul says, "Because there is one bread, we who are many are one body, for we all partake of the one bread" (1 Cor 10:17). Union with Christ is also union with all those to whom he gives himself. I cannot possess Christ just for myself; I can belong to him only in union with all those who have become, or who will become, his own. Communion draws me out of myself toward him, and thus also toward unity with all Christians. We become "one body", completely joined in a single existence. Love of God and love of neighbor are now truly united: God incar-

nate draws us all to himself. We can thus understand how *agape* also became a term for the Eucharist: there God's own *agape* comes to us bodily, in order to continue his work in us and through us. Only by keeping in mind this Christological and sacramental basis can we correctly understand Jesus' teaching on love. The transition which he makes from the Law and the Prophets to the twofold commandment of love of God and of neighbor, and his grounding the whole life of faith on this central precept, is not simply a matter of morality—something that could exist apart from and alongside faith in Christ and its sacramental re-actualization. Faith, worship and *ethos* are interwoven as a single reality which takes shape in our encounter with God's *agape*. Here the usual contraposition between worship and ethics simply falls apart. "Worship" itself, Eucharistic communion, includes the reality both of being loved and of loving others in turn. A Eucharist which does not pass over into the concrete practice of love is intrinsically fragmented. Conversely, as we shall have to consider in greater detail below, the "commandment" of love is only possible because it is more than a requirement. Love can be "commanded" because it has first been given.

FRIENDS OF JESUS CHRIST

Holy Thursday is the day on which the Lord gave the Twelve the priestly task of celebrating, in the bread and the wine, the Sacrament of his Body and Blood until he comes again. The paschal lamb and all the sacrifices of the Old Covenant are replaced by the gift of his Body and his Blood, the gift of himself.

Thus, the new worship was based on the fact that, in the first place, God makes a gift to us, and, filled with this gift, we become his: creation returns to the Creator.

So it is that the priesthood also became something new: it was no longer a question of lineage but of discovering oneself in the mystery of Jesus Christ. He is always the One who gives, who draws us to himself.

He alone can say: "This is my Body . . . this is my Blood." The mystery of the priesthood of the Church lies in the fact that we, miserable human beings, by virtue of the Sacrament, can speak with his "*I*": *in persona Christi*. He wishes to exercise *his* priesthood through us. On Holy Thursday, we remember in a special way this moving mystery, which moves us anew in every celebration of the Sacrament.

So that daily life will not dull what is great and mysterious, we need this specific commemoration, we need to return to that hour in which he placed his hands upon us and made us share in this mystery.

Let us reflect once again on the signs in which the Sacrament has been given to us. At the center is the very ancient rite of the imposition of hands, with which he took possession of me, saying to me: "You belong to me."

However, in saying this he also said: "You are under the protection of my hands. You are under the protection of my heart. You are kept safely in the palm of my hands, and this is precisely how you find yourself in the immensity of my love. Stay in my hands, and give me yours."

Then let us remember that our hands were anointed with oil, which is the sign of the Holy Spirit and his power. Why one's hands? The human hand is the instrument of human action, it is the symbol of the human capacity to face the world, precisely to "take it in hand".

The Lord has laid his hands upon us and he now wants our hands so that they may become his own in the world. He no longer wants them to be instruments for taking things, people or the world for ourselves, to reduce them to being our possession, but instead, by putting ourselves at the service of his love, they can pass on his divine touch.

He wants our hands to be instruments of service, hence, an expression of the mission of the whole person who vouches for him and brings him to men and women. If human hands symbolically represent human faculties and, in general, skill as power to dispose of the world, then anointed hands must be a sign of the human capacity for giving, for creativity in shaping the world with love. It is for this reason, of course, that we are in need of the Holy Spirit.

In the Old Testament, anointing is the sign of being taken into service: the king, the prophet, the priest, each does and gives more than what derives from himself alone. In a certain way, he is emptied of himself, so as to serve by making himself available to One who is greater than he.

If, in today's Gospel, Jesus presents himself as God's Anointed One, the Christ, then this itself means that he is acting for the Father's mission and in unity with the Holy Spirit. He is thereby giving the world a new kingship, a new priesthood, a new way of being a prophet who does not seek himself but lives for the One with a view to whom the world was created.

Today, let us once again put our hands at his disposal and pray to him to take us by the hand, again and again, and lead us.

In the sacramental gesture of the imposition of hands by the Bishop, it was the Lord himself who laid his hands upon us. This sacramental sign sums up an entire existential process.

Once, like the first disciples, we encountered the Lord and heard his words: "Follow me!" Perhaps, to start with, we followed him somewhat hesitantly, looking back and wondering if this really was the road for us. And at some point on the journey, we may have had the same experience as Peter after the miraculous catch; in other words, we may have been frightened by its size, by the size of the task and by the inadequacy of our own poor selves, so that we wanted to turn back. "Depart from me, for I am a sinful man, O Lord" (Lk 5:8).

Then, however, with great kindness, he took us by the hand, he drew us to himself and said to us: "Do not fear! I am with you. I will not abandon you, do not leave me!"

And more than just once, the same thing that happened to Peter may have happened to us: while he was walking on the water toward the Lord, he suddenly realized that the water was not holding him up and that he was beginning to sink. And like Peter we cried, "Lord, save me!" (Mt 14:30). Seeing the elements raging on all sides, how could we get through the roaring, foaming waters of the past century, of the past millennium?

But then we looked toward him . . . and he grasped us by the hand and gave us a new "specific weight": the lightness that derives from faith and draws us upward. Then he stretched out to us the hand that sustains and carries us. He supports us. Let us fix our gaze ever anew on him and reach out to him. Let us allow his hand to take ours, and then we will not sink but will serve the life that is stronger than death and the love that is stronger than hatred.

Faith in Jesus, Son of the living God, is the means through which, time and again, we can take hold of Jesus' hand and in which he takes our hands and guides us.

One of my favorite prayers is the request that the liturgy puts on the lips of the priest before Communion ". . . never let me be separated from you". Let us ask that we never fall away from communion with his Body, with Christ himself, that we do not fall away from the Eucharistic mystery. Let us ask that he will never let go of our hands. . . .

The Lord laid his hand upon us. He expressed the meaning of this gesture in these words: "No longer do I call you servants, for the servant does not know what his master is doing; but I have called you friends, for all that I have heard from my Father I have made known to you" (Jn 15:15).

I no longer call you servants but friends: in these words one could actually perceive the institution of the priesthood. The Lord makes us his friends; he entrusts everything to us; he entrusts himself to us, so that we can speak with he himself—*in persona Christi capitis.*

What trust! He has truly delivered himself into our hands. The essential signs of priestly ordination are basically all a manifestation of those words: the laying on of hands; the consignment of the book—of his words that he entrusts to us; the consignment of the chalice, with which he transmits to us his most profound and personal mystery.

The power to absolve is part of all this. It also makes us share in his awareness of the misery of sin and of all the darkness in the world, and places in our hands the key to reopen the door to the Father's house.

I no longer call you servants but friends. This is the profound meaning of being a priest: becoming the friend of Jesus Christ. For this friendship we must daily recommit ourselves.

Friendship means sharing in thought and will. We must put into practice this communion of thought with Jesus, as Saint Paul tells us in his Letter to the Philippians (cf. 2:2–5). And this communion of thought is not a purely intellectual thing, but a sharing of sentiments and will, hence, also of actions. This means that we should know Jesus in an increasingly personal way, listening to him, living together with him, staying with him.

Listening to him—in *lectio divina*, that is, reading Sacred Scripture in a non-academic but spiritual way; thus, we learn to encounter Jesus present, who speaks to us. We must reason and reflect, before him and with him, on his words and actions. The reading of Sacred Scripture is prayer, it must be prayer—it must emerge from prayer and lead to prayer.

The Evangelists tell us that the Lord frequently withdrew —for entire nights—"to the mountains", to pray alone. We too need these "mountains": they are inner peaks that we must scale, the mountain of prayer.

Only in this way does the friendship develop. Only in this way can we carry out our priestly service, only in this way can we take Christ and his Gospel to men and women.

Activism by itself can even be heroic, but in the end external action is fruitless and loses its effectiveness unless it is born from deep inner communion with Christ. The time we spend on this is truly a time of pastoral activity, authentic pastoral activity. The priest must above all be a man of prayer.

The world in its frenetic activism often loses its direction. Its action and capacities become destructive if they lack the power of prayer, from which flow the waters of life that irrigate the arid land.

I no longer call you servants, but friends. The core of the priesthood is being friends of Jesus Christ. Only in this way can we truly speak *in persona Christi*, even if our inner remoteness from Christ cannot jeopardize the validity of the Sacrament. Being a friend of Jesus, being a priest, means being a man of prayer. In this way we recognize him and emerge from the ignorance of simple servants. We thus learn to live, suffer and act with him and for him.

Being friends with Jesus is par excellence always friendship with his followers. We can be friends of Jesus only in communion with the whole of Christ, with the Head and with the Body; in the vigorous vine of the Church to which the Lord gives life.

Sacred Scripture is a living and actual Word, thanks to the Lord, only in her. Without the living subject of the Church that embraces the ages, more often than not the Bible would have splintered into heterogeneous writings and would thus have become a book of the past. It is eloquent in the present only where the "Presence" is—where Christ remains for ever contemporary with us: in the Body of his Church.

Being a priest means becoming an ever closer friend of Jesus Christ with the whole of our existence. The world needs God—not just any god but the God of Jesus Christ, the God who made himself flesh and blood, who loved us to the point of dying for us, who rose and created within himself room for man. This God must live in us and we in him. This is our priestly call: only in this way can our action as priests bear fruit.

I would like to end this Homily with a word on Andrea Santoro, the priest from the Diocese of Rome who was assassinated in Trebizond while he was praying.

Cardinal Cé recounted to us during the Spiritual Exercises what Fr Santoro said. It reads: "I am here to dwell among these people and enable Jesus to do so by lending him my flesh. . . . One becomes capable of salvation only by offering one's own flesh. The evil in the world must be borne and the pain shared, assimilating it into one's own flesh as did Jesus."

Jesus assumed our flesh; let us give him our own. In this way he can come into the world and transform it. Amen!

THE HOPE OF THE GRAIN OF WHEAT

On the eve of his Passion, during the Passover meal, the Lord took the bread in his hands—as we heard a short time ago in the Gospel passage—and, having blessed it, he broke it and gave it to his Disciples, saying: "Take this, this is my body". He then took the chalice, gave thanks and passed it to them and they all drank from it. He said: "This is my blood, the blood of the covenant, to be poured out on behalf of many" (Mk 14:22–24).

The entire history of God with humanity is recapitulated in these words. The past alone is not only referred to and interpreted, but the future is anticipated—the coming of the Kingdom of God into the world. What Jesus says are not simply words. What he says is an event, the central event of the history of the world and of our personal lives.

These words are inexhaustible. In this hour, I would like to meditate with you on just one aspect. Jesus, as a sign of his presence, chose bread and wine. With each one of the two signs he gives himself completely, not only in part. The Risen One is not divided. He is a person who, through signs, comes near to us and unites himself to us.

Each sign however, represents in its own way a particular aspect of his mystery and through its respective manifestation, wishes to speak to us so that we learn to understand the mystery of Jesus Christ a little better.

During the procession and in adoration we look at the

consecrated Host, the most simple type of bread and nourishment, made only of a little flour and water. In this way, it appears as the food of the poor, those to whom the Lord made himself closest in the first place.

The prayer with which the Church, during the liturgy of the Mass, consigns this bread to the Lord, qualifies it as fruit of the earth and the work of humans.

It involves human labor, the daily work of those who till the soil, sow and harvest [the wheat] and, finally, prepare the bread. However, bread is not purely and simply what we produce, something made by us; it is fruit of the earth and therefore is also gift.

We cannot take credit for the fact that the earth produces fruit; the Creator alone could have made it fertile. And now we too can expand a little on this prayer of the Church, saying: the bread is fruit of heaven and earth together. It implies the synergy of the forces of earth and the gifts from above, that is, of the sun and the rain. And water too, which we need to prepare the bread, cannot be produced by us.

In a period in which desertification is spoken of and where we hear time and again the warning that man and beast risk dying of thirst in these waterless regions—in such a period we realize once again how great is the gift of water and of how we are unable to produce it ourselves.

And so, looking closely at this little piece of white Host, this bread of the poor, appears to us as a synthesis of creation. Heaven and earth, too, like the activity and spirit of man, cooperate. The synergy of the forces that make the mystery of life and the existence of man possible on our poor planet come to meet us in all of their majestic grandeur.

In this way we begin to understand why the Lord chooses this piece of bread to represent him. Creation, with all of its gifts, aspires above and beyond itself to something even greater. Over and above the synthesis of its own forces, above and beyond the synthesis also of nature and of spirit that, in some way, we detect in the piece of bread, creation is projected toward divinization, toward the holy wedding feast, toward unification with the Creator himself.

And still, we have not yet explained in depth the message of this sign of bread. The Lord mentioned its deepest mystery on Palm Sunday, when some Greeks asked to see him. In his answer to this question is the phrase: "Truly, truly, I say to you, unless a grain of wheat falls into the earth and dies, it remains alone; but if it dies, it bears much fruit" (Jn 12:24).

The mystery of the Passion is hidden in the bread made of ground grain. Flour, the ground wheat, presuppose the death and resurrection of the grain. In being ground and baked, it carries in itself once again the same mystery of the Passion. Only through death does resurrection arrive, as does the fruit and new life.

Mediterranean culture, in the centuries before Christ, had a profound intuition of this mystery. Based on the experience of this death and rising they created myths of divinity which, dying and rising, gave new life. To them, the cycle of nature seemed like a divine promise in the midst of the darkness of suffering and death that we are faced with.

In these myths, the soul of the human person, in a certain way, reached out toward that God made man, who, humiliated unto death on a cross, in this way opened the door of life to all of us. In bread and its making, man has understood it as a waiting period of nature, like a promise of nature that this would come to exist: the God that dies and in this way brings us to life.

What was awaited in myths and that in the very grain of wheat is hidden like a sign of the hope of creation—this

truly came about in Christ. Through his gratuitous suffering and death, he became bread for all of us, and with this
living and certain hope. He accompanies us in all of our
sufferings until death. The paths that he travels with us and
through which he leads us to life are pathways of hope.

When, in adoration, we look at the consecrated Host,
the sign of creation speaks to us. And so, we encounter the
greatness of his gift; but we also encounter the Passion, the
Cross of Jesus and his Resurrection. Through this gaze of
adoration, he draws us toward himself, within his mystery,
through which he wants to transform us as he transformed
the Host.

The primitive Church discovered yet another symbol in
the bread. The Doctrine of the Twelve Apostles [*Didachē*],
a book written around the year 100, contains in its prayers
the affirmation: "Even as this broken bread was scattered
over the hills, and was gathered together and became one,
so let Thy Church be gathered together from the ends of
the earth into Thy Kingdom" (IX, 4).

Bread made of many grains contains also an event of
union: the ground grain becoming bread is a process of unification. We ourselves, many as we are, must become one
bread, one body, as Saint Paul says (cf. 1 Cor 10:17). In this
way the sign of bread becomes both hope and fulfillment.

In a very similar way the sign of wine speaks to us. However, while bread speaks of daily life, simplicity and pilgrimage, wine expresses the exquisiteness of creation: the feast of
joy that God wants to offer to us at the end of time and that
already now and always anticipates anew a foretaste through
this sign.

But, wine also speaks of the Passion: the vine must be re-
peatedly pruned to be purified in this way; the grapes must

mature with the sun and the rain and must be pressed: only through this passion does a fine wine mature.

On the feast of *Corpus Christi* we especially look at the sign of bread. It reminds us of the pilgrimage of Israel during the forty years in the desert. The Host is our manna whereby the Lord nourishes us—it is truly the bread of heaven, through which he gives himself.

In the procession we follow this sign and in this way we follow Christ himself. And we ask of him: Guide us on the paths of our history! Show the Church and her Pastors again and again the right path! Look at suffering humanity, cautiously seeking a way through so much doubt; look upon the physical and mental hunger that torments it! Give men and women bread for body and soul! Give them work! Give them light! Give them yourself! Purify and sanctify all of us! Make us understand that only through participation in your Passion, through "yes" to the cross, to self-denial, to the purifications that you impose upon us, our lives can mature and arrive at true fulfillment. Gather us together from all corners of the earth. Unite your Church, unite wounded humanity! Give us your salvation! Amen!

THE CHURCH AS
A EUCHARISTIC COMMUNITY

"You are Peter, and on this rock I will build my Church"
(Mt 16:18).

What exactly was the Lord saying to Peter with these
words? With them, what promise did he make to Peter and
what task did he entrust to him? And what is he saying to
us—to the Bishop of Rome, who is seated on the chair of
Peter, and to the Church today?

If we want to understand the meaning of Jesus' words, it
is useful to remember that the Gospels recount for us three
different situations in which the Lord, each time in a special
way, transmits to Peter his future task. The task is always
the same, but what the Lord was and is concerned with becomes clearer to us from the diversity of the situations and
images used.

In the Gospel according to Saint Matthew that we have
just heard, Peter makes his own confession to Jesus, recognizing him as the Messiah and Son of God. On the basis of
this, his special task is conferred upon him though three images: the rock that becomes the foundation or cornerstone,
the keys, and the image of binding and loosing.

I do not intend here to interpret once again these three
images that the Church down the ages has explained over
and over again; rather, I would like to call attention to the
geographical place and chronological context of these words.

The promise is made at the sources of the Jordan, on the boundary of the Judaic Land, on the frontiers of the pagan world. The moment of the promise marks a crucial turning-point in Jesus' journey: the Lord now sets out for Jerusalem and for the first time, he tells the disciples that this journey to the Holy City is the journey to the Cross: "From that time Jesus began to show his disciples that he must go to Jerusalem and suffer many things from the elders and chief priests and scribes, and be killed, and on the third day be raised" (Mt 16:21).

Both these things go together and determine the inner place of the Primacy, indeed, of the Church in general: the Lord is continuously on his way toward the Cross, toward the lowliness of the servant of God, suffering and killed, but at the same time he is also on the way to the immensity of the world in which he precedes us as the Risen One, so that the light of his words and the presence of his love may shine forth in the world; he is on the way so that through him, the Crucified and Risen Christ, God himself, may arrive in the world.

In this regard, Peter describes himself in his First Letter as "a witness of the sufferings of Christ as well as a partaker in the glory that is to be revealed" (1 Pt 5:1). For the Church, Good Friday and Easter have always existed together; she is always both the mustard seed and the tree in whose boughs the birds of the air make their nests.

The Church—and in her, Christ—still suffers today. In her, Christ is again and again taunted and slapped; again and again an effort is made to reject him from the world. Again and again the little barque of the Church is ripped apart by the winds of ideologies, whose waters seep into her and seem to condemn her to sink. Yet, precisely in the suffering Church, Christ is victorious.

In spite of all, faith in him recovers ever new strength. The Lord also commands the waters today and shows that he is the Lord of the elements. He stays in his barque, in the little boat of the Church.

Thus, on the one hand, the weakness proper to human beings is revealed in Peter's ministry, but at the same time, also God's power: in the weakness of human beings itself the Lord shows his strength; he demonstrates that it is through frail human beings that he himself builds his Church.

Let us now turn to the Gospel according to Saint Luke, which tells us that during the Last Supper, the Lord once again confers a special task upon Peter (cf. Lk 22:31–33). This time, the Lord's words addressed to Simon are found immediately after the Institution of the Most Blessed Eucharist. The Lord has just given himself to his followers under the species of bread and wine. We can see the Institution of the Eucharist as the true and proper founding act of the Church.

Through the Eucharist, the Lord not only gives himself to his own but also gives them the reality of a new communion among themselves which is extended in time, "until he comes" (cf. 1 Cor 11:26).

Through the Eucharist, the disciples become his living dwelling place which, as history unfolds, grows like the new and living temple of God in this world. Thus, immediately after the Institution of the Sacrament, Jesus speaks of what being disciples, of what the "ministry", means in the new community: he says that it is a commitment of service, just as he himself is among them as One who serves.

And then he addresses Peter. He says that Satan has demanded to have him so that he may sift him like wheat. This calls to mind the passage in the Book of Job, where Satan asks God for the power to afflict Job. The devil—the slanderer of God and men—thereby wants to prove that no true religious feeling exists, but that in man every aim is always solely utilitarian.

In the case of Job, God grants Satan the asked-for freedom precisely to be able by so doing to defend his creature—man —and himself. And this also happens with Jesus' disciples. God gives a certain liberty to Satan in all times.

To us it oftentimes seems that God allows Satan too much freedom, that he grants him the power to distress us too terribly; and that this gets the better of our forces and oppresses us too heavily. Again and again we cry out to God: "Alas, look at the misery of your disciples! Ah, protect us!" In fact, Jesus continues: "I have prayed for you that your faith may not fail" (Lk 22:32).

Jesus' prayer is the limit set upon the power of the devil. Jesus' prayer is the protection of the Church. We can seek refuge under this protection, cling on to it and be safe. But —as he says in the Gospel—Jesus prays in a particular way for Peter: ". . . that your faith may not fail".

Jesus' prayer is at the same time a promise and a duty. Jesus' prayer safeguards Peter's faith, that faith which he confessed at Caesarea Philippi: "You are the Christ, the Son of the living God" (Mt 16:16). And so, never let this faith be silenced; strengthen it over and over again, even in the face of the cross and all the world's contradictions: this is Peter's task.

Therefore, the point is that the Lord does not only pray for Peter's personal faith, but for his faith as a service to others. This is exactly what he means with the words: "When you have turned again, strengthen your brethren" (Lk 22:32).

"When you have turned again": these words are at the same time a prophecy and a promise. They prophesy the weakness of Simon, who was to deny to a maid and a servant that he knew Christ. Through this fall, Peter—and with him the Church of all times—has to learn that one's own strength alone does not suffice to build and guide the Lord's Church. No one succeeds on his or her own. However capable and clever Peter may seem—already at the first moment of trial he fails.

"When you have turned again": the Lord, who predicted his fall, also promises him conversion: "And the Lord turned and looked at Peter . . ." (Lk 22:61). Jesus' look works the transformation and becomes Peter's salvation: "he went out and wept bitterly" (Lk 22:62).

Let us implore ever anew this saving gaze of Jesus: for all those who have responsibility in the Church; for all who suffer the bewilderment of these times; for the great and for the small: Lord, look at us ever anew, pick us up every time we fall and take us in your good hands.

It is through the promise of his prayer that the Lord entrusts to Peter the task for the brethren. Peter's responsibility is anchored in Jesus' prayer. It is this that gives him the certainty that he will persevere through all human miseries.

And the Lord entrusts this task to him in the context of the Supper, in connection with the gift of the Most Holy Eucharist. The Church, established in the institution of the Eucharist, in her inmost self is a Eucharistic community, hence, communion in the Body of the Lord. Peter's task is to preside over this universal communion; to keep it present in the world also as visible, incarnate unity. He, together with the whole Church of Rome—as Saint Ignatius of Antioch said—, must preside in charity: preside over the community with that love which comes from Christ and ever anew surpasses the limitations of the private sphere to bring God's love to the ends of the earth.

The third reference to the Primacy is found in the Gospel

according to Saint John (21:15–19). The Lord is risen, and as the Risen One he entrusts his flock to Peter. Here too, the Cross and the Resurrection are interconnected. Jesus predicts to Peter that he is to take the way of the Cross. In this Basilica built over the tomb of Peter—a tomb of the poor —we see that in this very way the Lord, through the Cross, is always victorious. His power is not a power according to the ways of this world. It is the power of goodness: of truth and of love, which is stronger than death.

Yes, his promise is true: the powers of death, the gates of hell, will not prevail against the Church which he built on Peter (cf. Mt 16:18) and which he, in this very way, continues to build personally.

On this Solemnity of the Holy Apostles Peter and Paul, I address you especially, dear Metropolitans, who have come from many countries of the world to receive the Pallium from the Successor of Peter. I offer you a cordial greeting, together with all those who have accompanied you.

I also greet with special joy the delegation of the Ecumenical Patriarchate, led by His Eminence Ioannis Zizioulas, Metropolitan of Pergamon and President of the Joint International Commission for Theological Dialogue between the Catholics and the Orthodox. I am grateful to Patriarch Bartholomew I and to the Holy Synod for this sign of brotherhood that demonstrates the desire and the commitment to progress more swiftly on the path of full unity that Christ invoked for all his disciples. We feel we share the ardent desire, once expressed by Patriarch Athenagoras and Pope Paul VI, to drink together from the same Cup and to eat together the Bread which is the Lord himself. Let us implore once again on this occasion that this gift may soon be granted to us.

And let us thank the Lord that we are united in the confession Peter made on behalf of all the disciples at Caesarea Philippi: "You are the Christ, the Son of the living God." Let us together bring this confession to the contemporary world.

May the Lord help us at this very moment in our history to be true witnesses of the sufferings of Christ as well as partakers in the glory that is to be revealed (cf. 1 Pt 5:1). Amen!

GOD IS NOT FAR FROM US

The reading we have just heard is from the final book of the New Testament, the Book of Revelation. The seer is helped to lift his eyes upward, toward heaven, and forward, toward the future. But in doing so, he speaks to us about earth, about the present, about our lives. In the course of our lives, all of us are on a journey, we are traveling toward the future. Naturally, we want to find the right road: to find true life, and not a dead end or a desert. We don't want to end up saying: I took the wrong road, my life is a failure, it went wrong. We want to find joy in life; we want, in the words of Jesus, "to have life in abundance".

But let us listen to the seer of the Book of Revelation. What has he said to us in this passage which was read to us a moment ago? He is talking about a reconciled world. A world in which people "of every nation, race, people and tongue" (7:9) have come together in joy. And so we ask: "How can this happen? What road do we take to get there?" Well, first and most important: these people are living with God; God himself has "sheltered them in his tent" (cf. 7:15), as the reading says. So we ask ourselves again: "What do we mean by 'God's tent'? Where is it found? How do we get there?" The seer might be alluding to the first chapter of the Gospel according to John, where we read: "The Word became flesh and pitched his tent among us" (1:14). God is not far from us, he is not somewhere out in the universe, somewhere that none of us can go. He has pitched his tent among us: in Jesus he became one of us, flesh and blood just like us. This is his "tent". And in the Ascension, he did not go somewhere far away from us. His tent, he himself in his Body, remains among us and is one of us. We can call him by name and speak at ease with him. He listens to us and, if we are attentive, we can also hear him speaking back.

Let me repeat: In Jesus, it is God who "camps" in our midst. But let me also repeat: Where exactly does this happen? Our reading gives us two answers to this question. It says that the men and women at peace "have washed their robes and made them white in the blood of the Lamb" (7:14). To us this sounds very strange. In his cryptic language, the seer is speaking about Baptism. His words about "the blood of the Lamb" allude to Jesus' love, which he continued to show even up to his violent death. This love, both divine and human, is the bath into which he plunges us at Baptism —the bath with which he washes us, cleansing us so that we can be fit for God and capable of living in his company. The act of Baptism, however, is just a beginning. By walking with Jesus, in faith and in our life in union with him, his love touches us, purifies us and enlightens us. We heard that, in the bath of love, our clothing becomes white. For the ancient world, white was the color of light. The white robes mean that in faith we become light, we set aside darkness, falsehood and every sort of evil, and we become people of light, fit for God. The baptismal gown, like the First Communion robes that you are wearing, is meant to remind us of this, and to tell us: by living as one with Jesus and the community of believers, the Church, you have become a person of light, a person of truth and goodness—a person radiant with goodness, the goodness of God himself.

The second answer to the question: "Where do we find

Jesus?" is also given by the seer in cryptic language. He tells us that the Lamb leads the great multitude of people from every culture and nation to the sources of living water. Without water, there is no life. People who lived near the desert knew this well, and so springs of water became for them the symbol par excellence of life. The Lamb, Jesus, leads men and women to the sources of life. Among these sources are the Sacred Scriptures, in which God speaks to us and tells us the how to live in the right way. But there is more to these sources: in truth the authentic source is Jesus himself, in whom God gives us his very self. He does this above all in Holy Communion. There we can, as it were, drink directly from the source of life: he comes to us and makes each of us one with him. We can see how true this is: through the Eucharist, the sacrament of communion, a community is formed which spills over all borders and embraces all languages—we see it here: there are present Bishops of every language and from throughout the world—through communion the universal Church takes shape, in which God speaks to us and lives among us. This is how we should receive Holy Communion: seeing it as an encounter with Jesus, an encounter with God himself, who leads us to the sources of true life.

Dear parents! I ask you to help your children to grow in faith, I ask you to accompany them on their journey toward First Communion, a journey which continues beyond that day, and to keep accompanying them as they make their way to Jesus and with Jesus. Please, go with your children to Church and take part in the Sunday Eucharistic celebration! You will see that this is not time lost; rather, it is the very thing that can keep your family truly united and centered. Sunday becomes more beautiful, the whole week becomes more beautiful, when you go to Sunday Mass together. And please, pray together at home too: at meals and before going to bed. Prayer does not only bring us nearer to God but also nearer to one another. It is a powerful source of peace and joy. Family life becomes more joyful and expansive whenever God is there and his closeness is experienced in prayer.

Dear catechists and teachers! I urge you to keep alive in the schools the search for God, for that God who in Jesus Christ has made himself visible to us. I know that in our pluralistic world it is no easy thing in schools to bring up the subject of faith. But it is hardly enough for our children and young people to learn technical knowledge and skills alone, and not the criteria that give knowledge and skill their direction and meaning. Encourage your students not only to raise questions about particular things—something good in itself—, but above all to ask about the why and the wherefore of life as a whole. Help them to realize that any answers that do not finally lead to God are insufficient.

Dear priests and all who assist in parishes! I urge you to do everything possible to make the parish a "spiritual community" for people—a great family where we also experience the even greater family of the universal Church, and learn through the liturgy, through catechesis and through all the events of parish life to walk together on the way of true life.

These three places of education—the family, the school and the parish—go together, and they help us to find the way that leads to the sources of life, and truly all of us, dear children, dear parents and dear teachers, want to have "life in abundance". Amen!

SACRAMENT OF THE LIFE OF GOD

1. The sacrament of charity,[1] the Holy Eucharist is the gift that Jesus Christ makes of himself, thus revealing to us God's infinite love for every man and woman. This wondrous sacrament makes manifest that "greater" love which led him to "lay down his life for his friends" (Jn 15:13). Jesus did indeed love them "to the end" (Jn 13:1). In those words the Evangelist introduces Christ's act of immense humility: before dying for us on the Cross, he tied a towel around himself and washed the feet of his disciples. In the same way, Jesus continues, in the sacrament of the Eucharist, to love us "to the end", even to offering us his Body and his Blood. What amazement must the Apostles have felt in witnessing what the Lord did and said during that Supper! What wonder must the eucharistic mystery also awaken in our own hearts!

The food of truth

2. In the sacrament of the altar, the Lord meets us, men and women created in God's image and likeness (cf. Gen 1:27), and becomes our companion along the way. In this sacrament, the Lord truly becomes food for us, to satisfy our hunger for truth and freedom. Since only the truth can

[1] Cf. Saint Thomas Aquinas, *Summa Theologiae* III, q. 73, a. 3.

make us free (cf. Jn 8:32), Christ becomes for us the food of truth. With deep human insight, Saint Augustine clearly showed how we are moved spontaneously, and not by constraint, whenever we encounter something attractive and desirable. Asking himself what it is that can move us most deeply, the saintly Bishop went on to say: "What does our soul desire more passionately than truth?"[2] Each of us has an innate and irrepressible desire for ultimate and definitive truth. The Lord Jesus, "the way, and the truth, and the life" (Jn 14:6), speaks to our thirsting, pilgrim hearts, our hearts yearning for the source of life, our hearts longing for truth. Jesus Christ is the Truth in person, drawing the world to himself. "Jesus is the lodestar of human freedom: without him, freedom loses its focus, for without the knowledge of truth, freedom becomes debased, alienated and reduced to empty caprice. With him, freedom finds itself."[3] In the sacrament of the Eucharist, Jesus shows us in particular the *truth about the love* which is the very essence of God. It is this evangelical truth which challenges each of us and our whole being. For this reason, the Church, which finds in the Eucharist the very center of her life, is constantly concerned to proclaim to all, *opportune importune* (cf. 2 Tim 4:2), that God is love.[4] Precisely because Christ has become for us the food of truth, the Church turns to every man and woman, inviting them freely to accept God's gift.

---

[2] Saint Augustine, *In Iohannis Evangelium Tractatus*, 26,5: PL 35, 1609.

[3] Benedict XVI, Address to Participants in the Plenary Assembly of the Congregation for the Doctrine of the Faith (10 February 2006): AAS 98 (2006), 255.

[4] Benedict XVI, Address to the Members of the Ordinary Council of the General Secretariat of the Synod of Bishops (1 June 2006): *L'Osservatore Romano*, 2 June 2006, p. 5.

Figura transit in veritatem

11. Jesus thus brings his own radical *novum* to the ancient Hebrew sacrificial meal. For us Christians, that meal no longer need be repeated. As the Church Fathers rightly say, *figura transit in veritatem*: the foreshadowing has given way to the truth itself. The ancient rite has been brought to fulfillment and definitively surpassed by the loving gift of the incarnate Son of God. The food of truth, Christ sacrificed for our sake, *dat figuris terminum*.[5] By his command to "do this in remembrance of me" (Lk 22:19; 1 Cor 11:25), he asks us to respond to his gift and to make it sacramentally present. In these words the Lord expresses, as it were, his expectation that the Church, born of his sacrifice, will receive this gift, developing under the guidance of the Holy Spirit the liturgical form of the sacrament. The remembrance of his perfect gift consists not in the mere repetition of the Last Supper, but in the Eucharist itself, that is, in the radical newness of Christian worship. In this way, Jesus left us the task of entering into his "hour". "The Eucharist draws us into Jesus' act of self-oblation. More than just statically receiving the incarnate *Logos*, we enter into the very dynamic of his self-giving."[6] Jesus "draws us into himself."[7] The substantial conversion of bread and wine into his Body and Blood introduces within creation the principle of a radical change, a sort of "nuclear fission," to use an image familiar to us

[5] Roman Breviary, *Hymn for the Office of Readings of the Solemnity of Corpus Christi*.

[6] Benedict XVI, Encyclical Letter *Deus Caritas Est* (25 December 2005), 13: AAS 98 (2006), 228.

[7] Benedict XVI, Homily at Marienfeld Esplanade (21 August 2005): AAS 97 (2005), 891–92.

today, which penetrates to the heart of all being, a change meant to set off a process which transforms reality, a process leading ultimately to the transfiguration of the entire world, to the point where God will be all in all (cf. 1 Cor 15:28).

The Eucharist and the Virgin Mary

33. From the relationship between the Eucharist and the individual sacraments, and from the eschatological significance of the sacred mysteries, the overall shape of the Christian life emerges, a life called at all times to be an act of spiritual worship, a self-offering pleasing to God. Although we are all still journeying toward the complete fulfillment of our hope, this does not mean that we cannot already gratefully acknowledge that God's gifts to us have found their perfect fulfillment in the Virgin Mary, Mother of God and our Mother. Mary's Assumption body and soul into heaven is for us a sign of sure hope, for it shows us, on our pilgrimage through time, the eschatological goal of which the sacrament of the Eucharist enables us even now to have a foretaste.

In Mary most holy, we also see perfectly fulfilled the "sacramental" way that God comes down to meet his creatures and involves them in his saving work. From the Annunciation to Pentecost, Mary of Nazareth appears as someone whose freedom is completely open to God's will. Her immaculate conception is revealed precisely in her unconditional docility to God's word. Obedient faith in response to God's work shapes her life at every moment. A virgin attentive to God's word, she lives in complete harmony with his will; she treasures in her heart the words that come to her from God and, piecing them together like a mosaic, she learns to understand them more deeply (cf. Lk 2:19, 51); Mary is the great Believer who places herself confidently in God's hands, abandoning herself to his will.[8] This mystery deepens as she becomes completely involved in the redemptive mission of Jesus. In the words of the Second Vatican Council, "the blessed Virgin advanced in her pilgrimage of faith, and faithfully persevered in her union with her Son until she stood at the Cross, in keeping with the divine plan (cf. Jn 19:25), suffering deeply with her only-begotten Son, associating herself with his sacrifice in her mother's heart, and lovingly consenting to the immolation of the victim who was born of her. Finally, she was given by the same Christ Jesus, dying on the Cross, as a mother to his disciple, with these words: 'Woman, behold your Son.'"[9] From the Annunciation to the Cross, Mary is the one who received the Word, made flesh within her and then silenced in death. It is she, lastly, who took into her arms the lifeless body of the one who truly loved his own "to the end" (Jn 13:1).

Consequently, every time we approach the Body and Blood of Christ in the eucharistic liturgy, we also turn to her who, by her complete fidelity, received Christ's sacrifice for the whole Church. The Synod Fathers rightly declared that "Mary inaugurates the Church's participation in the sacrifice of the Redeemer."[10] She is the Immaculata, who receives God's gift unconditionally and is thus associated with his work of salvation. Mary of Nazareth, icon of the nascent Church, is the model for each of us, called to receive the gift that Jesus makes of himself in the Eucharist.

---

[8] Cf. Benedict XVI, Homily (8 December 2005): AAS 98 (2006), 15–16.

[9] Dogmatic Constitution on the Church *Lumen Gentium*, 58.

[10] *Propositio* 4.

Spiritual worship—logiké latreía (*Rom 12:1*)

70. The Lord Jesus, who became for us the food of truth and love, speaks of the gift of his life and assures us that "if any one eats of this bread, he will live for ever" (Jn 6:51). This "eternal life" begins in us even now, thanks to the transformation effected in us by the gift of the Eucharist: "He who eats me will live because of me" (Jn 6:57). These words of Jesus make us realize how the mystery "believed" and "celebrated" contains an innate power making it the principle of new life within us and the form of our Christian existence. By receiving the Body and Blood of Jesus Christ we become sharers in the divine life in an ever more adult and conscious way. Here too, we can apply Saint Augustine's words, in his *Confessions*, about the eternal *Logos* as the food of our souls. Stressing the mysterious nature of this food, Augustine imagines the Lord saying to him: "I am the food of grown men; grow, and you shall feed upon me; nor shall you change me, like the food of your flesh, into yourself, but you shall be changed into me." [11] It is not the eucharistic food that is changed into us, but rather we who are mysteriously transformed by it. Christ nourishes us by uniting us to himself; "he draws us into himself." [12]

Here the eucharistic celebration appears in all its power as the source and summit of the Church's life, since it expresses at once both the origin and the fulfillment of the new and

[11] VII, 10, 16: PL 32, 742.

[12] Benedict XVI, Homily at Marienfeld Esplanade (21 August 2005): AAS 97 (2005), 892; cf. Homily for the Vigil of Pentecost (3 June 2006): AAS 98 (2006), 505.

definitive worship of God, the *logiké latreía*.[13] Saint Paul's
exhortation to the Romans in this regard is a concise de-
scription of how the Eucharist makes our whole life a spiritual worship pleasing to God: "I appeal to you therefore,
my brothers, by the mercies of God, to present your bodies as a living sacrifice, holy and acceptable to God, which
is your spiritual worship" (Rom 12:1). In these words the
new worship appears as a total self-offering made in communion with the whole Church. The Apostle's insistence on
the offering of our bodies emphasizes the concrete human
reality of a worship which is anything but disincarnate. The
Bishop of Hippo goes on to say that "this is the sacrifice of
Christians: that we, though many, are one body in Christ.
The Church celebrates this mystery in the sacrament of the
altar, as the faithful know, and there she shows them clearly
that in what is offered, she herself is offered."[14] Catholic
doctrine, in fact, affirms that the Eucharist, as the sacrifice
of Christ, is also the sacrifice of the Church, and thus of
all the faithful.[15] This insistence on sacrifice—a "making
sacred"—expresses all the existential depth implied in the
transformation of our human reality as taken up by Christ
(cf. Phil 3:12).

The all-encompassing effect of eucharistic worship

71. Christianity's new worship includes and transfigures every aspect of life: "Whether you eat or drink, or whatever

---

[13] Cf. *Relatio post disceptationem*, 6, 47: *L'Osservatore Romano*, 14 October
2005, pp. 5–6; *Propositio* 43.

[14] *De Civitate Dei*, X, 6: PL 41, 284.

[15] Cf. *Catechism of the Catholic Church*, 1368.

you do, do all to the glory of God" (1 Cor 10:31). Christians, in all their actions, are called to offer true worship to God. Here the intrinsically eucharistic nature of Christian life begins to take shape. The Eucharist, since it embraces the concrete, everyday existence of the believer, makes possible, day by day, the progressive transfiguration of all those called by grace to reflect the image of the Son of God (cf. Rom 8:29ff.). There is nothing authentically human—our thoughts and affections, our words and deeds—that does not find in the sacrament of the Eucharist the form it needs to be lived to the full. Here we can see the full human import of the radical newness brought by Christ in the Eucharist: the worship of God in our lives cannot be relegated to something private and individual, but tends by its nature to permeate every aspect of our existence. Worship pleasing to God thus becomes a new way of living our whole life, each particular moment of which is lifted up, since it is lived as part of a relationship with Christ and as an offering to God. The glory of God is the living man (cf. 1 Cor 10:31). And the life of man is the vision of God.[16]

Iuxta dominicam viventes—
living in accordance with the Lord's Day

72. From the beginning Christians were clearly conscious of this radical newness which the Eucharist brings to human life. The faithful immediately perceived the profound influence of the eucharistic celebration on their manner of life. Saint Ignatius of Antioch expressed this truth when he

---

[16] Cf. Saint Irenaeus, *Adv. Haer.*, IV, 20, 7: PG 7, 1037.

called Christians "those who have attained a new hope", and described them as "those living in accordance with the Lord's Day" (*iuxta dominicam viventes*).[17] This phrase of the great Antiochene martyr highlights the connection between the reality of the Eucharist and everyday Christian life. The Christians' customary practice of gathering on the first day after the Sabbath to celebrate the resurrection of Christ— according to the account of Saint Justin Martyr[18]—is also what defines the form of a life renewed by an encounter with Christ. Saint Ignatius' phrase—"living in accordance with the Lord's Day"—also emphasizes that this holy day becomes paradigmatic for every other day of the week. Indeed, it is defined by something more than the simple suspension of one's ordinary activities, a sort of parenthesis in one's usual daily rhythm. Christians have always experienced this day as the first day of the week, since it commemorates the radical newness brought by Christ. Sunday is thus the day when Christians rediscover the eucharistic form which their lives are meant to have. "Living in accordance with the Lord's Day" means living in the awareness of the liberation brought by Christ and making our lives a constant self-offering to God, so that his victory may be fully revealed to all humanity through a profoundly renewed existence.

Living the Sunday obligation

73. Conscious of this new vital principle which the Eucharist imparts to the Christian, the Synod Fathers reaf-

---

[17] *Ad Magnes.*, 9, 1: PG 5, 670.
[18] Cf. *1 Apologia*, 67, 1–6; 66: PG 6, 430ff., 427, 430.

firmed the importance of the Sunday obligation for all the faithful, viewing it as a wellspring of authentic freedom enabling them to live each day in accordance with what they celebrated on "the Lord's Day". The life of faith is endangered when we lose the desire to share in the celebration of the Eucharist and its commemoration of the paschal victory. Participating in the Sunday liturgical assembly with all our brothers and sisters, with whom we form one body in Jesus Christ, is demanded by our Christian conscience and at the same time it forms that conscience. To lose a sense of Sunday as the Lord's Day, a day to be sanctified, is symptomatic of the loss of an authentic sense of Christian freedom, the freedom of the children of God.[19] Here some observations made by my venerable predecessor John Paul II in his Apostolic Letter *Dies Domini*[20] continue to have great value. Speaking of the various dimensions of the Christian celebration of Sunday, he said that it is *Dies Domini* with regard to the work of creation, *Dies Christi* as the day of the new creation and the Risen Lord's gift of the Holy Spirit, *Dies Ecclesiae* as the day on which the Christian community gathers for the celebration, and *Dies hominis* as the day of joy, rest and fraternal charity.

Sunday thus appears as the primordial holy day, when all believers, wherever they are found, can become heralds and guardians of the true meaning of time. It gives rise to the Christian meaning of life and a new way of experiencing time, relationships, work, life and death. On the Lord's Day, then, it is fitting that Church groups should organize, around Sunday Mass, the activities of the Christian community: so-

---

[19] Cf. *Propositio* 30.
[20] Cf. AAS 90 (1998), 713–66.

cial gatherings, programs for the faith formation of children, young people and adults, pilgrimages, charitable works, and different moments of prayer. For the sake of these important values—while recognizing that Saturday evening, beginning with First Vespers, is already a part of Sunday and a time when the Sunday obligation can be fulfilled—we need to remember that it is Sunday itself that is meant to be kept holy, lest it end up as a day "empty of God".[21]

The meaning of rest and of work

74. Finally, it is particularly urgent nowadays to remember that the day of the Lord is also a day of rest from work. It is greatly to be hoped that this fact will also be recognized by civil society, so that individuals can be permitted to refrain from work without being penalized. Christians, not without reference to the meaning of the Sabbath in the Jewish tradition, have seen in the Lord's Day a day of rest from their daily exertions. This is highly significant, for *it relativizes work* and directs it to the person: work is for man and not man for work. It is easy to see how this actually protects men and women, emancipating them from a possible form of enslavement. As I have had occasion to say, "work is of fundamental importance to the fulfillment of the human being and to the development of society. Thus, it must always be organized and carried out with full respect for human dignity and must always serve the common good. At the same time, it is indispensable that people not allow themselves to be enslaved by work or to idolize it, claiming

[21] *Propositio* 30.

to find in it the ultimate and definitive meaning of life."[22]
It is on the day consecrated to God that men and women
come to understand the meaning of their lives and also of
their work.[23]

97. Through the intercession of the Blessed Virgin Mary,
may the Holy Spirit kindle within us the same ardor experienced by the disciples on the way to Emmaus (cf. Lk
24:13–35) and renew our "eucharistic wonder" through
the splendor and beauty radiating from the liturgical rite,
the efficacious sign of the infinite beauty of the holy mystery of God. Those disciples arose and returned in haste to
Jerusalem in order to share their joy with their brothers and
sisters in the faith. True joy is found in recognizing that the
Lord is still with us, our faithful companion along the way.
The Eucharist makes us discover that Christ, risen from the
dead, is our contemporary in the mystery of the Church, his
body. Of this mystery of love we have become witnesses.
Let us encourage one another to walk joyfully, our hearts
filled with wonder, toward our encounter with the Holy
Eucharist, so that we may experience and proclaim to others the truth of the words with which Jesus took leave of
his disciples: "Lo, I am with you always, until the end of
the world" (Mt 28:20).

[22] Homily (19 March 2006): AAS 98 (2006), 324.

[23] The *Compendium of the Social Doctrine of the Church*, 258, rightly notes in
this regard: "For man, bound as he is to the necessity of work, this rest opens
to the prospect of a fuller freedom, that of the eternal Sabbath (cf. Heb 4:9–
10). Rest gives men and women the possibility to remember and experience
anew God's work, from Creation to Redemption, to recognize themselves
as his work (cf. Eph 2:10), and to give thanks for their lives and for their
subsistence to him who is their author."

EUCHARIST:
SOURCE AND SCHOOL OF LOVE

I have willingly come to pay you a Visit, and the most important moment of our meeting is Holy Mass, where the gift of God's love is renewed: a love that comforts us and gives us peace, especially in life's difficult moments.

In this prayerful atmosphere I would like to address my greeting to each one of you: to the Hon. Mr. Clemente Mastella, Minister of Justice, to whom I express a special "thank you"; to Mrs. Melìta Cavallo, Department Head of Justice for Minors, to the other Authorities who have spoken, to those in charge, to the operators, teachers and personnel of this juvenile penitentiary, to the volunteers, to your relatives and to everyone present.

I greet the Cardinal Vicar and Auxiliary Bishop Benedetto Túzia.

I greet in particular, Msgr. Giorgio Caniato, General Inspector of the Prisons Chaplaincy, and your Chaplain, whom I thank for expressing your sentiments at the beginning of Holy Mass.

In the Eucharistic celebration it is Christ himself who becomes present among us; indeed, even more: he comes to enlighten us with his teaching—in the Liturgy of the Word—and to nourish us with his Body and his Blood—in the Eucharistic Liturgy and in Communion.

Thus, he comes to teach us to love, to make us capable of loving and thereby capable of living. But perhaps you will say, how difficult it is to love seriously and to live well! What is the secret of love, the secret of life? Let us return to the Gospel [of the Prodigal Son].

In this Gospel three persons appear: the father and two sons. But these people represent two rather different life projects. Both sons lived peacefully, they were fairly well-off farmers so they had enough to live on, selling their produce profitably, and life seemed good.

Yet little by little the younger son came to find this life boring and unsatisfying: "All of life can't be like this", he thought: rising every day, say at six o'clock, then according to Israel's traditions, there must have been a prayer, a reading from the Holy Bible, then they went to work and at the end of the day another prayer.

Thus, day after day he thought: "But no, life is something more. I must find another life where I am truly free, where I can do what I like; a life free from this discipline, from these norms of God's commandments, from my father's orders; I would like to be on my own and have life with all its beauties totally for myself. Now, instead, it is nothing but work. . . ."

And so he decided to claim the whole of his share of his inheritance and leave. His father was very respectful and generous and respected the son's freedom: it was he who had to find his own life project. And he departed, as the Gospel says, to a far-away country. It was probably geographically distant because he wanted a change, but also inwardly distant because he wanted a completely different life.

So his idea was: freedom, doing what I want to do, not recognizing these laws of a God who is remote, not being in the prison of this domestic discipline, but rather doing what is beautiful, what I like, possessing life with all its beauty and fullness.

And at first—we might imagine, perhaps for a few months —everything went smoothly: he found it beautiful to have attained life at last, he felt happy.

Then, however, little by little, he felt bored here, too; here too everything was always the same. And in the end, he was left with an emptiness that was even more disturbing: the feeling that this was still not life became ever more acute; indeed, going ahead with all these things, life drifted further and further away. Everything became empty: the slavery of doing the same things then also re-emerged. And in the end, his money ran out and the young man found that his standard of living was lower than that of swine.

It was then that he began to reflect and wondered if that really was the path to life: a freedom interpreted as doing what I want, living, having life only for me; or if instead it might be more of a life to live for others, to contribute to building the world, to the growth of the human community. . . .

So it was that he set out on a new journey, an inner journey. The boy pondered and considered all these new aspects of the problem and began to see that he had been far freer at home, since he had also been a landowner contributing to building his home and society in communion with the Creator, knowing the purpose of his life and guessing the project that God had in store for him.

During this interior journey, during this development of a new life project and at the same time living the exterior journey, the younger son was motivated to return, to start his life anew because he now understood that he had taken the wrong track. I must start out afresh with a different concept, he said to himself; I must begin again.

And he arrived at the home of the father who had left him his freedom to give him the chance to understand inwardly what life is and what life is not. The father embraced him with all his love, he offered him a feast and life could start again beginning from this celebration.

The son realized that it is precisely work, humility and daily discipline that create the true feast and true freedom. So he returned home, inwardly matured and purified: he had understood what living is.

Of course, in the future his life would not be easy either, temptations would return, but he was henceforth fully aware that life without God does not work; it lacks the essential, it lacks light, it lacks reason, it lacks the great sense of being human. He understood that we can only know God on the basis of his Word.

We Christians can add that we know who God is from Jesus, in whom the face of God has been truly shown to us. The young man understood that God's Commandments are not obstacles to freedom and to a beautiful life, but sign-posts on the road on which to travel to find life.

He realized too that work and the discipline of being committed, not to oneself but to others, extends life. And precisely this effort of dedicating oneself through work gives depth to life, because one experiences the pleasure of having at last made a contribution to the growth of this world that becomes freer and more beautiful.

I do not wish at this point to speak of the other son who stayed at home, but in his reaction of envy we see that inwardly he too was dreaming that perhaps it would be far better to take all the freedoms for himself. He too in his heart was "returning home" and understanding once again what life is, understanding that it is truly possible to live only with God, with his Word, in the communion of one's own family, of work; in the communion of the great Family of God.

I do not wish to enter into these details now: let each one of us apply this Gospel to himself in his own way. Our situations are different and each one has his own world. Nonetheless, the fact remains that we are all moved and that we can all enter with our inner journey into the depths of the Gospel.

Only a few more remarks: the Gospel helps us understand who God truly is. He is the Merciful Father who in Jesus loves us beyond all measure.

The errors we commit, even if they are serious, do not corrode the fidelity of his love. In the Sacrament of Confession we can always start out afresh in life. He welcomes us, he restores to us our dignity as his children.

Let us therefore rediscover this sacrament of forgiveness that makes joy well up in a heart reborn to true life.

Furthermore, this parable helps us to understand who the human being is: he is not a "monad", an isolated being who lives only for himself and must have life for himself alone.

On the contrary, we live with others, we were created together with others and only in being with others, in giving ourselves to others, do we find life.

The human being is a creature in whom God has impressed his own image, a creature who is attracted to the horizon of his Grace, but he is also a frail creature exposed to evil but also capable of good. And lastly, the human being is a free person.

We must understand what freedom is and what is only the appearance of freedom.

Freedom, we can say, is a springboard from which to dive

into the infinite sea of divine goodness, but it can also become a tilted plane on which to slide toward the abyss of sin and evil and thus also to lose freedom and our dignity.

Dear friends, we are in the *Season of Lent*, the forty days before Easter. In this Season of Lent, the Church helps us to make this interior journey and invites us to conversion, which always, even before being an important effort to change our behavior, is an opportunity to decide to get up and set out again, to abandon sin and to choose to return to God.

Let us—this is the imperative of Lent—make this journey of inner liberation together.

Every time, such as today, that we participate in the Eucharist, the source and school of love, we become capable of living this love, of proclaiming it and witnessing to it with our life.

Nevertheless, we need to decide to walk toward Jesus as the Prodigal Son did, returning inwardly and outwardly to his father.

At the same time, we must abandon the selfish attitude of the older son who was sure of himself, quick to condemn others and closed in his heart to understanding, acceptance and forgiveness of his brother, and who forgot that he too was in need of forgiveness.

May the Virgin Mary and Saint Joseph, my Patron Saint whose Feast it will be tomorrow, obtain this gift for us; I now invoke him in a special way for each one of you and for your loved ones.

THE PASSION OF JESUS

In the Reading from the Book of Exodus which we have just heard, the celebration of the Passover of Israel is described, just as in Mosaic Law it found its definitive form.

At the outset, it might have been a spring feast for nomads. For Israel, however, it was transformed into a commemorative feast of thanksgiving and, at the same time, hope.

The center of the Passover meal, regulated by specific liturgical provisions, was the lamb as the symbol of Israel's redemption from slavery in Egypt.

For this reason the paschal *haggada* was an integral part of the Passover meal based on lamb: the narrative commemoration of the fact that it had been God himself who set Israel free by "stretching out his hand".

He, the mysterious and hidden God, had shown himself to be stronger than Pharaoh, in spite of all the power that Pharaoh could muster.

Israel was never to forget that God had personally taken the history of his People in hand and that this history was based permanently on communion with God. Israel must not forget God.

The words of the commemoration were surrounded by words of praise and thanksgiving taken from the Psalms. Thanking and blessing God reached its culmination in the *berakha*, which in Greek is *eulogia* or *eucharistia*: praising God becomes a blessing for those who bless him. The offering given to God comes back blessed to man.

All this built a bridge from the past to the present and toward the future: Israel had not yet been liberated. The nation was still suffering, like a small people, in the sphere of tension between the great powers.

Thus, remembering with gratitude God's past action became at the same time supplication and hope: Bring to completion what you have begun! Grant us freedom once and for all!

It was on the eve of his Passion that Jesus together with his disciples celebrated this meal with its multiple meanings. This is the context in which we must understand the new Passover which he has given to us in the Blessed Eucharist.

There is an apparent discrepancy in the Evangelists' accounts, between John's Gospel on the one hand, and what on the other Matthew, Mark and Luke tell us.

According to John, Jesus died on the Cross at the very moment when the Passover lambs were being sacrificed in the temple. The death of Jesus and the sacrifice of the lambs coincided. However, this means that he must have died the day before Easter and could not, therefore, have celebrated the Passover meal in person—this, at any rate, is how it appears.

According to the three Synoptic Gospels, the Last Supper of Jesus was instead a Passover meal into whose traditional form he integrated the innovation of the gift of his Body and Blood.

This contradiction seemed unsolvable until a few years ago. The majority of exegetes were of the opinion that John was reluctant to tell us the true historical date of Jesus' death, but rather chose a symbolic date to highlight the deeper truth: Jesus is the new, true Lamb who poured out his Blood for us all.

In the meantime, the discovery of the [Dead Sea] Scrolls

at Qumran has led us to a possible and convincing solution which, although it is not yet accepted by everyone, is a highly plausible hypothesis. We can now say that John's account is historically precise.

Jesus truly shed his blood on the eve of Easter at the time of the immolation of the lambs. In all likelihood, however, he celebrated the Passover with his disciples in accordance with the Qumran calendar, hence, at least one day earlier; he celebrated it without a lamb, like the Qumran community which did not recognize Herod's temple and was waiting for the new temple.

Consequently, Jesus celebrated the Passover without a lamb—no, not without a lamb: instead of the lamb he gave himself, his Body and his Blood. Thus, he anticipated his death in a manner consistent with his words: "No one takes [my life] from me, but I lay it down of my own accord" (Jn 10:18).

At the time when he offered his Body and his Blood to the disciples, he was truly fulfilling this affirmation. He himself offered his own life. Only in this way did the ancient Passover acquire its true meaning.

In his Eucharistic catecheses, Saint John Chrysostom once wrote: Moses, what are you saying? Does the blood of a lamb purify men and women? Does it save them from death? How can the blood of an animal purify people, save people or have power over death? In fact, Chrysostom continues, the immolation of the lamb could be a merely symbolic act, hence, the expression of expectation and hope in One who could accomplish what the sacrifice of an animal was incapable of accomplishing.

The Lamb and Temple

Jesus celebrated the Passover without a lamb and without a temple; yet, not without a lamb and not without a temple. He himself was the awaited Lamb, the true Lamb, just as John the Baptist had foretold at the beginning of Jesus' public ministry: "Behold, the Lamb of God, who takes away the sin of the world!" (Jn 1:29).

And he himself was the true Temple, the living Temple where God dwells and where we can encounter God and worship him. His Blood, the love of the One who is both Son of God and true man, one of us, is the Blood that can save. His love, that love in which he gave himself freely for us, is what saves us. The nostalgic, in a certain sense, ineffectual gesture which was the sacrifice of an innocent and perfect lamb, found a response in the One who for our sake became at the same time Lamb and Temple.

Thus, the Cross was at the center of the new Passover of Jesus. From it came the new gift brought by him, and so it lives on for ever in the Blessed Eucharist in which, down the ages, we can celebrate the new Passover with the Apostles.

From Christ's Cross comes the gift. "No one takes [my life] from me, but I lay it down of my own accord." He now offers it to us.

The paschal *haggada*, the commemoration of God's saving action, has become a memorial of the Cross and Resurrection of Christ—a memorial that does not simply recall the past but attracts us within the presence of Christ's love.

Thus, the *berakha*, Israel's prayer of blessing and thanksgiving, has become our Eucharistic celebration in which the Lord blesses our gifts—the bread and wine—to give himself in them. Let us pray to the Lord that he will help us to understand this marvelous mystery ever more profoundly, to love it more and more, and in it, to love the Lord himself ever more.

Let us pray that he will increasingly draw us to himself with Holy Communion. Let us pray that he will help us not to keep our life for ourselves but to give it to him and thus to work with him so that people may find life: the true life which can only come from the One who himself is the Way, the Truth and the Life. Amen.

THE GIFT OF THE
SELF-DEDICATION OF CHRIST

We have just sung the Sequence: *"Dogma datur christianis, /
quod in carnem transit panis, / et vinum in sanguinem*—this [is]
the truth each Christian learns, / bread into his flesh he turns,
to his precious blood the wine."

Today we reaffirm with great joy our faith in the Eucharist, the Mystery that constitutes the heart of the Church.
In the recent Post-Synodal Apostolic Exhortation *Sacramentum Caritatis* I recalled that the Eucharistic Mystery "is the
gift that Jesus Christ makes of himself, thus revealing to us
God's infinite love for every man and woman" (no. 1).

Corpus Christi, therefore, is a unique feast and constitutes
an important encounter of faith and praise for every Christian community. This feast originated in a specific historical
and cultural context: it was born for the very precise purpose
of openly reaffirming the faith of the People of God in Jesus
Christ, alive and truly present in the Most Holy Sacrament
of the Eucharist. It is a feast that was established in order to
publicly adore, praise and thank the Lord, who continues
"to love us 'to the end', even to offering us his body and
his blood" (*Sacramentum Caritatis*, no. 1).

The Eucharistic celebration this evening takes us back
to the spiritual atmosphere of Holy Thursday, the day on
which in the Upper Room, on the eve of his Passion, Christ
instituted the Most Holy Eucharist.

Corpus Christi is thus a renewal of the mystery of Holy Thursday, as it were, in obedience to Jesus' invitation to proclaim from "the housetops" what he told us in secret (cf. Mt 10:27). It was the Apostles who received the gift of the Eucharist from the Lord in the intimacy of the Last Supper, but it was destined for all, for the whole world. This is why it should be proclaimed and exposed to view: so that each one may encounter "Jesus who passes" as happened on the roads of Galilee, Samaria and Judea; in order that each one, in receiving it, may be healed and renewed by the power of his love. Dear friends, this is the perpetual and living heritage that Jesus has bequeathed to us in the Sacrament of his Body and his Blood. It is an inheritance that demands to be constantly rethought and relived so that, as venerable Pope Paul VI said, its "inexhaustible effectiveness may be impressed upon all the days of our mortal life" (cf. *Insegnamenti*, 25 May 1967, p. 779).

Also in the Post-Synodal Exhortation, commenting on the exclamation of the priest after the consecration: "*Let us proclaim the mystery of faith!*", I observed: with these words he "proclaims the mystery being celebrated and expresses his wonder before the substantial change of bread and wine into the Body and Blood of the Lord Jesus, a reality which surpasses all human understanding" (no. 6).

Precisely because this is a mysterious reality that surpasses our understanding, we must not be surprised if today too many find it hard to accept the Real Presence of Christ in the Eucharist. It cannot be otherwise. This is how it has been since the day when, in the synagogue at Capernaum, Jesus openly declared that he had come to give us his flesh and his blood as food (cf. Jn 6:26–58).

This seemed "a hard saying" and many of his disciples withdrew when they heard it. Then, as now, the Eucharist remains a *"sign of contradiction"* and can only be so because a God who makes himself flesh and sacrifices himself for the life of the world throws human wisdom into crisis.

However, with humble trust, the Church makes the faith of Peter and the other Apostles her own and proclaims with them, and we proclaim: "Lord, to whom shall we go? You have the words of eternal life" (Jn 6:68). Let us too renew this evening our profession of faith in Christ, alive and present in the Eucharist. Yes, *"this [is] the truth each Christian learns, / bread into his flesh he turns, / to his precious blood the wine."*

At its culminating point, in the Sequence we sing: *"Ecce panis angelorum, / factus cibus viatorum: / vere panis filiorum"* — "Lo! The angel's food is given / to the pilgrim who has striven; / see the children's bread from heaven." And by God's grace we are the children.

The Eucharist is the food reserved for those who in Baptism were delivered from slavery and have become sons; it is the food that sustained them on the long journey of the exodus through the desert of human existence.

Like the manna for the people of Israel, for every Christian generation the Eucharist is the indispensable nourishment that sustains them as they cross the desert of this world, parched by the ideological and economic systems that do not promote life but rather humiliate it. It is a world where the logic of power and possessions prevails rather than that of service and love; a world where the culture of violence and death is frequently triumphant.

Yet Jesus comes to meet us and imbues us with certainty: he himself is "the Bread of life" (Jn 6:35, 48). He repeated this to us in the words of the Gospel Acclamation: "I am the living bread from heaven, if any one eats of this bread, he will live for ever" (cf. Jn 6:51).

In the Gospel passage just proclaimed, Saint Luke, narrating the miracle of the multiplication of the five loaves and two fish with which Jesus fed the multitude "in a lonely place", concludes with the words: "And all ate and were satisfied" (cf. Lk 9:11–17).

I would like in the first place to emphasize this "all". Indeed, the Lord desired every human being to be nourished by the Eucharist, because the Eucharist is for everyone.

If the close relationship between the Last Supper and the mystery of Jesus' death on the Cross is emphasized on Holy Thursday, today, the Feast of *Corpus Christi*, with the procession and unanimous adoration of the Eucharist, attention is called to the fact that Christ sacrificed himself for all humanity. His passing among the houses and along the streets of our city will be for those who live there an offering of joy, eternal life, peace and love.

In the Gospel passage, a second element catches one's eye: the miracle worked by the Lord contains an explicit invitation to each person to make his own contribution. The two fish and five loaves signify our contribution, poor but necessary, which he transforms into a gift of love for all.

"Christ continues today" I wrote in the above-mentioned Post-Synodal Exhortation, "to exhort his disciples to become personally engaged" (*Sacramentum Caritatis*, no. 88).

Thus, the Eucharist is a call to holiness and to the gift of oneself to one's brethren: "Each of us is truly called, together with Jesus, to be bread broken for the life of the world" (*ibid.*).

Our Redeemer addressed this invitation in particular to us, dear brothers and sisters of Rome, gathered round the Eucharist in this historical square.

I greet you all with affection. My greeting is addressed first of all to the Cardinal Vicar and to the Auxiliary Bishops, to my other venerable Brother Cardinals and Bishops, as well as to the numerous priests and deacons, men and women religious and the many lay faithful.

At the end of the Eucharistic celebration we will join in the procession as if to carry the Lord Jesus in spirit through all the streets and neighborhoods of Rome. We will immerse him, so to speak, in the daily routine of our lives, so that he may walk where we walk and live where we live.

Indeed we know, as the Apostle Paul reminded us in his Letter to the Corinthians, that in every Eucharist, also in the Eucharist this evening, we "proclaim the Lord's death until he comes" (cf. 1 Cor 11:26). We travel on the highways of the world knowing that he is beside us, supported by the hope of being able to see him one day face to face, in the definitive encounter.

In the meantime, let us listen to his voice repeat, as we read in the Book of Revelation, "Behold, I stand at the door and knock; if any one hears my voice and opens the door, I will come in to him and eat with him, and he with me" (Rev 3:20).

The Feast of *Corpus Christi* wants to make the Lord's knocking audible, despite the hardness of our interior hearing. Jesus knocks at the door of our heart and asks to enter not only for the space of a day but for ever. Let us welcome him joyfully, raising to him with one voice the invocation of the Liturgy:

"*Very bread, Good Shepherd, tend us, / Jesu, of your love befriend us. . . . / You who all things can and know, / who on earth such food bestow, / grant us with your saints, though lowest, / where the heav'nly feast you show, / fellow heirs and guests to be.*"

Amen!

THE SOUL OF SUNDAY

"*Sine dominico non possumus!*" Without the gift of the Lord, without the Lord's day, we cannot live: That was the answer given in the year 304 by Christians from Abitene in present-day Tunisia, when they were caught celebrating the forbidden Sunday Eucharist and brought before the judge. They were asked why they were celebrating the Christian Sunday Eucharist, even though they knew it was a capital offense. "*Sine dominico non possumus*": in the word *dominicum/dominico* two meanings are inextricably intertwined, and we must once more learn to recognize their unity. First of all there is the gift of the Lord—this gift is the Lord himself: the Risen one, whom the Christians simply need to have close and accessible to them, if they are to be themselves. Yet this accessibility is not merely something spiritual, inward and subjective: the encounter with the Lord is inscribed in time on a specific day. And so it is inscribed in our everyday, corporal and communal existence, in temporality. It gives a focus, an inner order to our time and thus to the whole of our lives. For these Christians, the Sunday Eucharist was not a commandment, but an inner necessity. Without him who sustains our lives, life itself is empty. To do without or to betray this focus would deprive life of its very foundation, would take away its inner dignity and beauty.

Does this attitude of the Christians of that time apply also to us who are Christians today? Yes, it does, we too need a relationship that sustains us, that gives direction and content to our lives. We too need access to the Risen one, who sustains us through and beyond death. We need this encounter which brings us together, which gives us space for freedom, which lets us see beyond the bustle of everyday life to God's creative love, from which we come and toward which we are traveling.

Of course, if we listen to today's Gospel, if we listen to what the Lord is saying to us, it frightens us: "Whoever of you does not renounce all that he has and all links with his family cannot be my disciple." We would like to object: What are you saying, Lord? Isn't the family just what the world needs? Doesn't it need the love of father and mother, the love between parents and children, between husband and wife? Don't we need love for life, the joy of life? And don't we also need people who invest in the good things of this world and build up the earth we have received, so that everyone can share in its gifts? Isn't the development of the earth and its goods another charge laid upon us? If we listen to the Lord more closely, and above all if we listen to him in the context of everything he is saying to us, then we understand that Jesus does not demand the same from everyone. Each person has a specific task, to each is assigned a particular way of discipleship. In today's Gospel, Jesus is speaking directly of the specific vocation of the Twelve, a vocation not shared by the many who accompanied Jesus on his journey to Jerusalem. The Twelve must first of all overcome the scandal of the Cross, and then they must be prepared truly to leave everything behind; they must be prepared to assume the seemingly absurd task of traveling to the ends of the earth and, with their minimal education, proclaiming the Gospel of Jesus Christ to a world filled with claims to erudition and with real or apparent education—and naturally also to the poor and the simple. They must themselves be prepared to suffer martyrdom in the course of their journey into the vast world, and thus to bear witness to the Gospel of the Crucified and Risen Lord. If Jesus' words on this journey to Jerusalem, on which a great crowd accompanies him, are addressed in the first instance to the Twelve, his call naturally extends beyond the historical moment into all subsequent centuries. He calls people of all times to count exclusively on him, to leave everything else behind, so as to be totally available for him, and hence totally available for others: to create oases of selfless love in a world where so often only power and wealth seem to count for anything. Let us thank the Lord for giving us men and women in every century who have left all else behind for his sake, and have thus become radiant signs of his love. We need only think of people like Benedict and Scholastica, Francis and Clare of Assisi, Elizabeth of Hungary and Hedwig of Silesia, Ignatius of Loyola, Teresa of Avila, and in our own day, Mother Teresa and Padre Pio. With their whole lives, these people have become a living interpretation of Jesus' teaching, which through their lives becomes close and intelligible to us. Let us ask the Lord to grant to people in our own day the courage to leave everything behind and so to be available to everyone.

Yet if we now turn once more to the Gospel, we realize that the Lord is not speaking merely of a few individuals and their specific task; the essence of what he says applies to everyone. The heart of the matter he expresses elsewhere in these words: "For whoever would save his life will lose it; and whoever loses his life for my sake, he will save it. For what does it profit a man if he gains the whole world and loses or forfeits himself?'' (Lk 9:24f.). Whoever wants to keep his life just for himself will lose it. Only by giving ourselves do we receive our life. In other words: only the one who loves discovers life. And love always demands going out of oneself, it always demands leaving oneself. Anyone who looks just to himself, who wants the other only for himself, will lose both himself and the other. Without this profound losing of oneself, there is no life. The restless craving for life, so widespread among people today, leads to the barrenness of a lost life. ''Whoever loses his life for my sake . . .'', says the Lord: a radical letting-go of our self is only possible if in the process we end up, not by falling into the void, but into the hands of Love eternal. Only the love of God, who loses himself for us and gives himself to us, makes it possible for us also to become free, to let go, and so truly to find life. This is the heart of what the Lord wants to say to us in the seemingly hard words of this Sunday's Gospel. With his teaching he gives us the certainty that we can build on his love, the love of the incarnate God. Recognition of this is the wisdom of which today's reading speaks to us. Once again, we find that all the world's learning profits us nothing unless we learn to live, unless we discover what truly matters in life.

"*Sine dominico non possumus!*" Without the Lord and without the day that belongs to him, life does not flourish. Sunday has been transformed in our Western societies into the week-end, into leisure time. Leisure time is something good and necessary, especially amid the mad rush of the modern world; each of us knows this. Yet if leisure time lacks an inner focus, an overall sense of direction, then ultimately it becomes wasted time that neither strengthens nor builds us up. Leisure time requires a focus—the encounter with him who is our origin and goal. My great predecessor in the see of Munich and Freising, Cardinal Faulhaber, once put it like this: Give the soul its Sunday, give Sunday its soul.

Because Sunday is ultimately about encountering the risen Christ in word and sacrament, its span extends through the whole of reality. The early Christians celebrated the first day of the week as the Lord's day, because it was the day of the resurrection. Yet very soon, the Church also came to realize that the first day of the week is the day of the dawning of creation, the day on which God said: "Let there be light" (Gen 1:3). Therefore Sunday is also the Church's weekly feast of creation—the feast of thanksgiving and joy over God's creation. At a time when creation seems to be endangered in so many ways through human activity, we should consciously advert to this dimension of Sunday too. Then, for the early Church, the first day increasingly assimilated the traditional meaning of the seventh day, the Sabbath. We participate in God's rest, which embraces all of humanity. Thus we sense on this day something of the freedom and equality of all God's creatures.

In this Sunday's Opening Prayer we call to mind firstly that through his Son God has redeemed us and made us his beloved children. Then we ask him to look down with loving-kindness upon all who believe in Christ and to give us true freedom and eternal life. We ask God to look down with loving-kindness. We ourselves need this look of loving-kindness not only on Sunday but beyond, reaching into our everyday lives. As we ask, we know that this loving gaze has already been granted to us. What is more, we know that God has adopted us as his children, he has truly welcomed us into communion with himself. To be someone's child means, as the early Church knew, to be a free person, not a slave but a member of the family. And it means being an heir. If we belong to God, who is the power above all powers, then we are fearless and free. And then we are heirs. The inheritance he has bequeathed to us is himself, his love. Yes, Lord, may this inheritance enter deep within our souls so that we come to know the joy of being redeemed. Amen.

TO STAND BEFORE YOU
AND TO SERVE

Every year the Chrism Mass exhorts us to enter into that "yes" to God's call, which we pronounced on the day of our priestly ordination. "*Adsum*—here I am!'", we have said like Isaiah, when he heard God's voice asking: "Whom shall I send, and who will go for us?" "Here am I! Send me", Isaiah responded (Is 6:8). Then the Lord himself, through the hands of the Bishop, placed his hands on us and we gave ourselves to his mission. Subsequently, we have followed many ways in the range of his call. Can we always affirm what Paul wrote to the Corinthians after years of Gospel service, often marked by fatigue and suffering of every type: "Our zeal has not slackened in this ministry which has been entrusted to us by God's mercy" (cf. 2 Cor 4:1)? "Our zeal has not slackened." Let us pray on this day that it may always be kindled anew, that it may be ever nourished by the living flame of the Gospel.

At the same time Holy Thursday is an occasion for us to ask ourselves over and over again: to what did we say our "yes"? What does this "being a priest of Jesus Christ" mean? The Second Canon of our Missal, which was probably compiled in Rome already at the end of the second century, describes the essence of the priestly ministry with the words with which, in the Book of Deuteronomy (18:5, 7), the essence of the Old Testament priesthood is described: *astare coram te et tibi ministrare* ["to stand and minister in the name of the Lord"]. There are therefore two duties that define the essence of the priestly ministry: in the first place, "to stand in his [the Lord's] presence." In the Book of Deuteronomy this is read in the context of the preceding disposition, according to which priests do not receive any portion of land in the Holy Land—they live of God and for God. They did not attend to the usual work necessary to sustain daily life. Their profession was to "stand in the Lord's presence"— to look to him, to be there for him. Hence, ultimately, the word indicated a life in God's presence, and with this also a ministry of representing others. As the others cultivated the land, from which the priest also lived, so he kept the world open to God, he had to live with his gaze on him. Now if this word is found in the Canon of the Mass immediately after the consecration of the gifts, after the entrance of the Lord in the assembly of prayer, then for us this points to being before the Lord present, that is, it indicates the Eucharist as the center of priestly life. But here too, the meaning is deeper. During Lent the hymn that introduces the Office of Readings of the Liturgy of the Hours—the Office that monks once recited during the night vigil before God and for humanity—one of the duties of Lent is described with the imperative: *arctius perstemus in custodia*— we must be even more intensely alert. In the tradition of Syrian monasticism, monks were qualified as "those who remained standing". This standing was an expression of vigilance. What was considered here as a duty of the monks, we can rightly see also as an expression of the priestly mission and as a correct interpretation of the word of Deuteronomy: the priest must be on the watch. He must be on his guard in the face of the imminent powers of evil.

He must keep the world awake for God. He must be

the one who remains standing: upright before the trends of time. Upright in truth. Upright in the commitment for good. Being before the Lord must always also include, at its depths, responsibility for humanity to the Lord, who in his turn takes on the burden of all of us to the Father. And it must be a taking on of him, of Christ, of his word, his truth, his love. The priest must be upright, fearless and prepared to sustain even offenses for the Lord, as referred to in the Acts of the Apostles: they were "rejoicing that they were counted worthy to suffer dishonor for the name" (5:41) of Jesus.

Now let us move on to the second word that the Second Canon repeats from the Old Testament text—"to stand in your presence and serve you". The priest must be an upright person, vigilant, a person who remains standing. Service is then added to all this. In the Old Testament text this word has an essentially ritualistic meaning: all acts of worship foreseen by the Law are the priests' duty. But this action, according to the rite, was classified as service, as a duty of service, and thus it explains in what spirit this activity must take place. With the assumption of the word "serve" in the Canon, the liturgical meaning of this term was adopted in a certain way—to conform with the novelty of the Christian cult. What the priest does at that moment, in the Eucharistic celebration, is to serve, to fulfill a service to God and a service to humanity. The cult that Christ rendered to the Father was the giving of himself to the end for humanity. Into this cult, this service, the priest must insert himself. Thus, the word "serve" contains many dimensions. In the first place, part of it is certainly the correct celebration of the liturgy and of the sacraments in general, accomplished through interior participation. We must learn to increasingly understand the sacred liturgy in all its essence, to develop a living familiarity with it, so that it becomes the soul of our daily life. It is then that we celebrate in the correct way; it is then that the *ars celebrandi*, the art of celebrating, emerges by itself. In this art there must be nothing artificial. If the liturgy is the central duty of the priest, this also means that prayer must be a primary reality, to be learned ever anew and ever more deeply at the school of Christ and of the Saints of all the ages. Since the Christian liturgy by its nature is also always a proclamation, we must be people who are familiar with the Word of God, love it and live by it: only then can we explain it in an adequate way. "To serve the Lord"— priestly service precisely also means to learn to know the Lord in his Word and to make it known to all those he entrusts to us.

Lastly, two other aspects are part of service. No one is closer to his master than the servant who has access to the most private dimensions of his life. In this sense "to serve" means closeness, it requires familiarity. This familiarity also bears a danger: when we continually encounter the sacred it risks becoming habitual for us. In this way, reverential fear is extinguished. Conditioned by all our habits we no longer perceive the great, new and surprising fact that he himself is present, speaks to us, gives himself to us. We must ceaselessly struggle against this becoming accustomed to the extraordinary reality, against the indifference of the heart, always recognizing our insufficiency anew and the grace that there is in the fact that he consigned himself into our hands. To serve means to draw near, but above all it also means obedience. The servant is under the word: "not my will, but thine, be done" (Lk 22:42). With this word Jesus, in the Garden of Olives, has resolved the decisive battle against sin, against the rebellion of the sinful heart. Adam's sin consisted precisely in the fact that he wanted to accomplish his own will and not God's. Humanity's temptation is always to want to be totally autonomous, to follow its own will alone and to maintain that only in this way will we be free; that only thanks to a similarly unlimited freedom would man be completely man. But this is precisely how we pit ourselves against the truth. Because the truth is that we must share our freedom with others and we can be free only in communion with them. This shared freedom can be true freedom only if we enter into what constitutes the very measure of freedom, if we enter into God's will. This fundamental obedience that is part of the human being—a person cannot be merely for and by himself—becomes still more concrete in the priest: we do not preach ourselves, but him and his Word, which we could not have invented ourselves. We proclaim the Word of Christ in the correct way only in communion with his Body. Our obedience is a believing with the Church, a thinking and speaking with the Church, serving through her. What Jesus predicted to Peter also always applies: "You will be taken where you do not want to go." This letting oneself be guided where one does not want to be led is an essential dimension of our service, and it is exactly what makes us free. In this being guided, which can be contrary to our ideas and plans, we experience something new—the wealth of God's love.

"To stand in his presence and serve him": Jesus Christ as the true High Priest of the world has conferred to these words a previously unimaginable depth. He, who as Son was and is the Lord, has willed to become that Servant of God which the vision of the Book of the Prophet Isaiah had foreseen. He has willed to be the Servant of all. He has portrayed the whole of his high priesthood in the gesture of the washing of the feet. With the gesture of love to the end he washes our dirty feet, with the humility of his service he purifies us from the illness of our pride. Thus, he makes us able to become partakers of God's banquet. He has descended, and the true ascent of man is now accomplished in our descending with him and toward him. His elevation is the Cross. It is the deepest descent and, as love pushed to the end, it is at the same time the culmination of the ascent, the true "elevation" of humanity. "To stand in his presence and serve him": this now means to enter into his call to serve God. The Eucharist as the presence of the descent and ascent of Christ thus always recalls, beyond itself, the many ways of service through love of neighbor. Let us ask the Lord on this day for the gift to be able to say again in this sense our "yes" to his call: "Here am I! Send me" (Is 6:8). Amen.

ACKNOWLEDGMENTS

THE BREAD OF LIFE

Mass and Eucharistic Procession on the Solemnity of
  Corpus Domini
Homily of His Holiness Benedict XVI
Square before the Basilica of Saint John Lateran, Thursday,
  26 May 2005

L'Osservatore Romano, 1 June 2005, no. 22, p. 3
http://www.vatican.va/holy_father/benedict_xvi/homilies/
2005/documents/hf_ben-xvi_hom_20050526_corpus-domini
_en.html

WITHOUT SUNDAY WE CANNOT LIVE

Pastoral Visit of His Holiness Benedict XVI to Bari for the
  Closing of the 24th Italian National Eucharistic Congress
Esplanade of Marisabella, Sunday, 29 May 2005

L'Osservatore Romano, 1 June 2005, no. 22, pp. 6–7
http://www.vatican.va/holy_father/benedict_xvi/homilies/
2005/documents/hf_ben-xvi_hom_20050529_bari_en.html

MARY, THE EUCHARISTIC WOMAN

Address of His Holiness Benedict XVI During the Prayer
  Meeting in the Vatican Gardens for the Conclusion of the
  Marian Month of May

Grotto of Our Lady of Lourdes in the Vatican Gardens,
   Tuesday, 31 May 2005

L'Osservatore Romano, 8 June 2005, no. 23, p. 2
http://www.vatican.va/holy_father/benedict_xvi/speeches/
2005/may/documents/hf_ben-xvi_spe_20050531_rosary-
may_en.html

IN THE HOUR OF JESUS

Apostolic Journey to Cologne on the Occasion of the
   Twentieth World Youth Day Eucharistic Celebration
Homily of His Holiness Pope Benedict XVI
Cologne—Marienfeld, Sunday, 21 August 2005

L'Osservatore Romano, 24 August 2005, no. 34, pp. 11–12
http://www.vatican.va/holy_father/benedict_xvi/homilies/
2005/documents/hf_ben-xvi_hom_20050821_20th-world-
youth-day_en.html

THE WINE OF TRUE LOVE

Opening Mass of the Eleventh Ordinary General Assembly
   of the Synod of Bishops
Homily of His Holiness Benedict XVI
Vatican Basilica, Sunday, 2 October 2005

L'Osservatore Romano, 5 October 2005, no. 40, pp. 6–7
http://www.vatican.va/holy_father/benedict_xvi/homilies/
2005/documents/hf_ben-xvi_hom_20051002_opening-
synod-bishops_en.html

THE EUCHARIST AS THE WAY TO HOLINESS

Conclusion of the Eleventh Ordinary General Assembly
   of the Synod of Bishops and Year of the Eucharist
Canonization of the Blesseds:

Józef Bilczewski
Gaetano Catanoso
Zygmunt Gorazdowski
Alberto Hurtado Cruchaga
Felix of Nicosta

Homily of His Holiness Benedict XVI
Saint Peter's Square, World Mission Sunday, 23 October
2005

L'Osservatore Romano, 26 October 2005, no. 43, pp. 1,
16–17
http://www.vatican.va/holy_father/benedict_xvi/homilies/
2005/documents/hf_ben-xvi_hom_20051023_canonizations
_en.html

JESUS CHRIST: INCARNATE LOVE OF GOD

Encyclical Letter *Deus Caritas Est* of the Supreme
Pontiff Benedict XVI to the Bishops Priests and Deacons,
Men and Women Religious and All the Lay Faithful
on Christian Love
Given in Rome, at Saint Peter's, on 25 December, the
Solemnity of the Nativity of the Lord, in the year 2005

Benedict XVI, *God Is Love*, Vatican translation (San
Francisco: Ignatius Press, 2006), 35–38
http://www.vatican.va/holy_father/benedict_xvi/encycli
cals/documents/hf_ben-xvi_enc_20051225_deus-caritas-est
_en.html

FRIENDS OF JESUS CHRIST

Chrism Mass in Saint Peter's Basilica
Homily of His Holiness Benedict XVI
Holy Thursday, 13 April 2006

L'Osservatore Romano, 13 September 2006, no. 37, p. 7
http://www.vatican.va/holy_father/benedict_xvi/homilies/
2006/documents/hf_ben-xvi_hom_20060910_vespers-
munich_en.html

SACRAMENT OF THE LIFE OF GOD

Post-Synodal Apostolic Exhortation *Sacramentum Caritatis*
   of the Holy Father Benedict XVI to the Bishops, Clergy,
   Consecrated Persons and the Lay Faithful on the Eucharist
   as the Source and Summit of the Church's Life and
   Mission
Given in Rome, at Saint Peter's, on 22 February, the Feast
   of the Chair of Peter, in the year 2007

http://www.vatican.va/holy_father/benedict_xvi/apost_
exhortations/documents/hf_ben-xvi_exh_20070222_
sacramentum-caritatis_en.html

EUCHARIST: SOURCE AND SCHOOL OF LOVE

Visit to Rome's Prison for Minors, "Casal del Marmo"
Homily of His Holiness Benedict XVI
Chapel of the Merciful Father, Fourth Sunday of Lent,
   18 March 2007

L'Osservatore Romano, 21 March 2007, no. 12, p. 1
http://www.vatican.va/holy_father/benedict_xvi/homilies/
2007/documents/hf_ben-xvi_hom_20070318_istituto-
penitenziario_en.html

THE PASSION OF JESUS

Mass of the Lord's Supper 2007
Pope Benedict XVI

L'Osservatore Romano, 11 April 2007, no. 15, p. 3
http://www.ewtn.com/library/PAPALDOC/b16Lord
Sup07.htm

THE GIFT OF THE SELF-DEDICATION OF CHRIST

Holy Mass and Eucharistic Procession to the Basilica of
    Saint Mary Major on the Solemnity of Corpus Christi
Homily of His Holiness Benedict XVI
Square in front of the Basilica of Saint John Lateran,
    Thursday, 7 June 2007

L'Osservatore Romano, 13 June 2007, no. 24, pp. 6–7
http://www.vatican.va/holy_father/benedict_xvi/homilies/
2007/documents/hf_ben-xvi_hom_20070607_corpus-
christi_en.html

THE SOUL OF SUNDAY

Apostolic Journey of His Holiness Benedict XVI to Austria
    on the Occasion of the 850th Anniversary of the
    Foundation of the Shrine of Mariazell Eucharistic
    Celebration
Homily of His Holiness Benedict XVI
Saint Stephen's Cathedral, Vienna, Sunday, 9 September
    2007

L'Osservatore Romano, 12 September 2007, no. 37, p. 8
http://www.vatican.va/holy_father/benedict_xvi/homilies/
2007/documents/hf_ben-xvi_hom_20070909_wien_en.html

TO STAND BEFORE YOU AND TO SERVE

Chrism Mass
Homily of His Holiness Benedict XVI
Saint Peter's Basilica, Holy Thursday, 20 March 2008

L'Osservatore Romano, 26 March 2008, no. 13, p. 2
http://www.vatican.va/holy_father/benedict_xvi/homilies/
2008/documents/hf_ben-xvi_hom_20080320_messa-
crismale_en.html